Creative
Candlemaking

Other Books by the Author

PLASTICS AS DESIGN FORM
PLASTICS AS AN ART FORM
WAX AS ART FORM

Inspired by natural shapes, imagination created these candle forms — a strange creature by Donovan of California that has some resemblance to an owl; behind it, a candle patterned like a pinecone; next, another somewhat-owl jacketed in sand-filled polyester, and, on the right, a version of a fairytale mushroom.

Plain, hand-dipped candles in an elaborate wrought-iron candelabrum.

All these surface effects were built into the structure of these candles — pouring at angles, a carved hurricane candle that is filled, a casting of crumpled foil and colored wax, and layers of wax topped with whipped wax for this dessert celebration.

Unusual candles — rolled beeswax, combed wax, cupcake forms, and coils of wax.

Creative Candlemaking

by THELMA R. NEWMAN

CROWN PUBLISHERS, INC.

New York

To all the anonymous candlemakers
of yesterday and today who have
given so much to this craft

© 1972 by Thelma R. Newman

Library of Congress Catalog Card Number: 77-185071
ISBN: 0-517-NO 8192

Designed by Ruth Smerechniak

Printed in the United States of America

Published simultaneously in Canada by General Publishing Company Limited

Third Printing, November, 1972

ACKNOWLEDGMENTS

A source book such as this owes its being to countless anonymous craftsmen of yesterday and today. Their creative work is a gift to the public domain. Institutions such as the Metropolitan Museum of Art, the Museum of Contemporary Crafts, the Heraclean Museum provided useful resources in books and pictures.

Special thanks go to the following unselfish candlemakers who gave of their time to provide information and candle designs, with an added embrace to those * who demonstrated their candlemaking processes: George Arold, Kenneth Hamilton,* George and Irene Kinzie, Emily McGowan,* Floss Perisho, Bill Stone, Betty Thomforde,* Lee Weber,* and Barbara and Eric Zelman.* And to Norm Smith who meticulously processed my photographs, I am extremely grateful for a job well done.

Most of all, continuing thanks go to my husband Jack and sons Jay and Lee for helping in every aspect of writing this book; their contribution is inestimable and deeply felt.

T.R.N.

All photographs by the author unless otherwise credited.

Contents

PREFACE

After writing *Plastics as an Art Form* and *Plastics as Design Form,* both complex textbooks deeply involved with technology and professional application of polymer science to fine art and industrial design, my friends asked me in a somewhat denigrating manner why I was writing *Creative Candlemaking.* It took me aback because I see candlemaking (this grew out of my research for *Wax as Art Form*) as an old and venerable craft. Knowing about wax is a science; making a sound candle is craftsmanship; producing a beautiful design form is art; understanding candlemaking past and present is to know civilizations as they progressed; and researching the candle as folklore is to know the romance of the candle. Few subjects can compete in terms of breadth, depth, and discovery.

My research took me to all known books on candlemaking, back to the eighteenth century, and in my travels I have collected distinguished candles from Yugoslavia, Greece, Crete, Spain, Italy, Austria, England, Scandinavia, Israel, and America. Over 170 different candle designs are described.

But more than description, I was committed to detailing the complete candlemaking field—from its history and its rudiments to professional techniques used today in making candles. Today, most pamphlets and books on candlemaking seem to be sponsored by suppliers who are in the business of selling equipment and materials. Enough information is provided in those publications to lead the craftsman to making a sound and attractive candle, but there is always a dependence on the supplier for supplies. Esoteric names are used to describe common materials, and new knowledge coming from the field of plastics is presented ambiguously in small, expensive packages. I have dipped into my knowledge of plastics to bring to *Creative Candlemaking* the most relevant additions in additives and in mold materials—uncommitted to any commercial enterprise, even though brands are recommended for expediency.

Naturally, as a sculptor, I look at the candle form as a sculptor would, and, with a tendency toward being a purist about the use of materials and shapes, I want to see a material look like what it is and find it very distasteful to see wax imitate wood, marble, feathers, and fabrics. My selection of candle forms is predicated on that prejudice.

All the material within this book projects itself into the realm of possibility toward the serendipitous and creative exercise of good design. A chapter on designing candles crystallizes possibilities, and all candlemaking possibilities are presented in an open-ended way to further more personal expression in candlemaking. I see *Creative Candlemaking* not so much as a definitive statement about the craft and design of candles (and it is that), but as a launching pad toward ever more fruitful discoveries in the design and technology of candles.

Candlemaking has an anonymous tradition. Many beautiful candle designs are sold that way in shops. Since candles are not difficult to make, candle designs are not difficult to imitate either and original sources for an initial idea have become lost in a myriad of candle possibilities. Only where it was possible to pinpoint a creative source did I give credits. Many of the designs were mine; some designs take what appear to be imitative directions because process and technique repeated produce similarities. Because of the anonymity of those creative people who invented and originated the nameless candles shown within I dedicate my book to them.

1

It's not alone this candle I stick,
But my love's heart I mean to prick,
Whether he be asleep or awake,
I'll have him come to me and speke.

—ENGLISH FOLKLORE

Candlemaking as History

SO IT WAS SPOKEN until as recently as the early nineteenth century in the north of England. And the romantic candle is still with us today, despite much more expedient and efficient lighting devices. Candles still have such decorative, religious, and utilitarian appeal that the United States alone consumes over 40 million pounds of paraffin for candlemaking annually.

Although there is no record of the earliest candle or its first users, the candle's history strangely parallels human progress. Some authorities attribute the first candles to the Egyptians. Clay candleholders of the fourth century B.C. have been found in Egypt; and Tutankhamen's tomb contained a candleholder, a bronze socket on a wooden block. It is reported, too, that Teta, first king of the

Sixth Dynasty, used candleholders of conventional design. Discovering candleholders in Crete, Sir Arthur Evans states in *Palace of Minos* that the object "was surely intended for a stick of superfine material such as wax."

A very simple candle form attributed to the Romans by Pliny was a flax rope soaked in pitch and wax called a "link." Indeed, the candle derives its name from the Latin *candere,* meaning "to shine." Perhaps this early candle evolved from the use of resinous torches and the discovery that some wood fibers and vines could be pulled apart and then twisted into a long-burning torch—and still later, soaked in resins, pitch, and waxes—to make the first candles. A distinction should be made between candles and the early torches, splinters, and rushlights. These did not have

1

TABLE OF CANDLE EVENTS

13th century.	In Paris, the guild of traveling candlemakers went from house to house making candles.
15th century.	Sieur de Brex of Paris introduced the wood mold method of making candles—before that candles were dipped.
18th century.	Spermaceti, a crystalline substance from the head of the sperm whale, was used in candlemaking. One candlepower is based on the light given by one pure spermaceti candle weighing one-sixth of a pound, burning at a rate of 120 grams per hour.
1800–1855.	Candle-molding machines developed, comprising prototypes of today's molding machines.
1811.	Michel Chevreul discovered fat-splitting separation of natural fats into fatty acids and glycerin, leading to the use of stearin as a low-cost candle dilutent and constituent.
1825.	Cambacères introduced the plaited or braided wick of twisted cotton or linen yarn. Before this, wicks had to be snuffed because of accumulated carbon; the plaited wick bends over and allows ashes to drop down and be consumed.
1825.	**Michel Chevreul and Gay-Lussac took out a patent to manufacture stearic acid.**
1830.	Paraffin: Reisebach's use of hydrocarbons of the marsh grass series.
1831.	**De Milly improved on Chevreul and Gay-Lussac's method by substituting sodium salt with calcium hydroxide. Candles made by this method are called "Milly" candles.**
1834.	Morgan developed the continuous wicking machine.
Before 1847.	Palmer invented a wick that had one-tenth of the strands coated with nitrate of bismuth that caused the burned end of the wick to curl over.
1850.	James Young of Scotland introduced paraffin for the manufacture of candles (paraffin came from the petroleum seeps of Derbyshire).
1854.	Stearin (5–10 percent) and paraffin combined to make stronger, stiffer candles.
1859.	First drilling for oil.

a wick; the candle does, and it ranks very high in the scale of invention. It appeared in civilizations when conditions of social advance required its use.

In early eastern civilization, the Chinese and Japanese molded candles in paper tubes, using the wax of an insect called "Cocus" and the seeds of certain trees. Later, the Japanese made wicks of rolled-up rice paper. Their candle could then fit into the sharp spur of an iron or bronze candleholder, which is still in use today. In India, candles of animal wax were prohibited by religious decree, but wax was skimmed from boiling cinnamon and made into tapers for temple use and ceremony. The first candle remnant found in the Western world was discovered in a tiny French village dating from about the first century A.D. And along the northwest coast of America, Indians used the oily candlefish as a light source. The fish was inserted into the Y of a slit stick and lighted. In Shetland, wicks were also forced down the throats of a sea bird, the stormy petrel, into their fatty bodies and lighted.

Candles were early associated with religious

The very fine shape of these Sub-Minoan eleventh-century B.C. candleholders suggests that a material such as wax was used for lighting. *Courtesy Heraclean Archeological Museum, Heraclean, Crete*

observances, and this has been carried forward to contemporary religious practice. At the beginning of the Reformation, one church in Wittenberg is said to have consumed over twelve tons of candles per year in its 174 candelabra, holding 8,730 candles. In fact, church tithes were payable in beeswax.

The pre-Christian belief that souls of the dead take the form of the bee and that bees come from paradise still marks tradition. It was a pagan custom in ancient Rome to burn candles during the last days of December to symbolize the returning power of the sun. Perhaps King Arthur's first Yule feast, fifteen centuries ago, stemmed from that custom. The Greeks dedicated bees to the goddess Diana. And a wedding procession with torches accompanied the Greek bride to her new home where the mother and mother-in-law started the fire on the family hearth with them.

Ancient custom decreed that a candle be lighted at death so that demons could not approach and seize the soul of the dying. A Greek funeral custom was to light a torch to accompany the dead Hellene to his last home. The Romans adopted this custom, and tapers were used in the medieval funeral. To this day, candles burn around the Catholic bier.

Fire has always been regarded by man as symbolic of divine providence. Vesta, Roman goddess of the hearth, guarded the flame.

Candlemas (February 2) is the day when lessons are drawn from the candle as a symbol of burning love toward Christ. Candles have been blessed on that day since the eleventh century. Some Christians still use candles on the Christmas tree, and as we continue to light candles on our birthday cakes, we can trace this tradition back to the medieval practice of placing a taper in the hands of a child at baptism.

We can still picture choirboys singing the psalms by candlelight, as tradition tells us; and the carolers of the Isle of Man sang until their candles stopped burning. Folk custom has many symbolic practices—the Croatian child lights his candle from one held by his father; German wives leave lighted candles for the passing angels; Scandinavians leave candles burning for "Kristine" who brings gifts; and in Ireland, the youngest child, or a daughter named Mary, lights the candles at Christmastime. To remember the anniversary of a loved one, Jewish mourners light a candle contained in a glass.

Close to the body of religion weaves superstition. Candles could predict anything from weather to lovers, to safety and good fortune. They could also portend evil and transmit suffering to unlucky ones. When candle flames snapped, burned unsteadily or with a dim light, people watched for rain and wind.

3

This brass portable candleholder on a velvet covered shaft dates back to the sixteenth century. This example is at Wroxton College in Wroxton, England (formerly Wroxton Abbey).

Detail of the candle housing shows that the candle always pivots to an upright position even when the shaft is held at an angle.

Or when the candle burned blue, ghosts walked. At feast time in west Jutland the candle that burned longest foretold the longest life. In Scotland, a candle burning out before midnight foretold impending misfortune. In Scandinavia, the oldest member of the family, usually the father, extinguished Christmas candles at sunrise and made the sign of the cross over animals with the remaining wax to keep them healthy; fed some wax to fowl to increase their offspring; coated plows with it to make furrows straighter.

If a woman hated a man or sought revenge, all she had to do was thrust pins into a candle while reciting this poetic spell:

As I pierce this candle through
With my pins so sharp and true
May he torments feel and woe,
Worse and worse each moment grow.
And as candle burns away
May he languish and decay.
May the winding-sheet appear,
And his death thus show is near.
Let each pin play deadly part,
Writhe his limbs and stab his heart.

The author of these sweet lines probably was not skillful enough to fashion an honest-to-goodness wax effigy.

Curiously, in medieval times the bee was regarded as a model of industry, purity, and chastity—because it worked hard, produced offspring, and yet, it was thought, retained its virginity. People then did not know the function of the queen bee or that working bees are male. In some parts of England and France, peasants held that if a girl could blow into a dying flame and respark it, she was a virgin, but if it went out she was not. This custom harked back to the vestal virgins who, because of their pure life, might blow upon the Holy Fire. A match that was a slender wick of twisted cotton covered with wax and tipped with a flammable paste, used in colonial days, was called a vesta.

As late as the nineteenth century, peasants of Northumberland, England, practiced the custom of lighting candles to keep witches at bay on Allhallowmas Eve (Halloween). Indeed, we still frighten away witches, but with tongue in check. The legend said that witches would gather at Malkin Tower (a farmhouse in the Pendle Forest of Lancashire) and if the candles burned, one could keep them from working evil. These conferring witches did not take this lightly though; they tried to blow out the candles and if they succeeded, woe would befall the victim. But if lucky ones could succeed in keeping their candles burning till midnight the witches dispersed, defeated.

Lancashire people were not the only ones knowledgeable about the powers of the beeswax candle. Natives of the Andaman Islands in the Bay of Bengal kept evil spirits away from their forest with black beeswax. And if one of the islanders wanted harm to fall upon an enemy, he would burn beeswax, and his goddess of storms, Biliku, would wreak havoc on his foe.

Perhaps, too, the unpleasant odor of tallow (predominantly used for candles in times past because it was cheaper) would be just too ugly for evil spirits when burning in quantity. Beeswax, almost universally, became the material for church and temple candles. Whether it was because the virgin bees came to earth directly from heaven or whether bees had magical properties, it is a custom followed to this day that church candles shall contain more than 50 percent of virgin beeswax.

One of the oldest customs that persists in isolated parts of the Balkans, e.g., Salamis, Greece, is the making of grandfather candles, burned before and during Lent. I purchased some in the old Turkish market of Skoplje, Yugoslavia, before its devastating earthquake. People call it the grandfather candle because these candles are lighted for dead grandparents on Clean Monday, the first Monday of Lent, and are kept burning throughout the period of Lent—usually until Pentecost. The candles are taken to church on the appropriate day and lighted during the services and then are taken home and kept burning before the icons. Each thread of the candle represents one departed soul, and the number of threads is the same as that of the deceased. Thus, three threads would represent three dead.

This candle display from the Cathedral at Monserrat, near Barcelona, Spain, could have been seen in the same form centuries ago. Note the elegant pinched wax design, a traditional Spanish candle. Tons of candles are consumed each year in these churches to commemorate the dead or to pray for an event.

This grandfather candle made in the city of Skoplje, Yugoslavia, dates back to early Catholic church tradition. The candle is lighted for dead grandparents the first Monday of Lent and kept burning throughout the period of Lent until Pentecost. Each thread of the wick represents one departed soul.

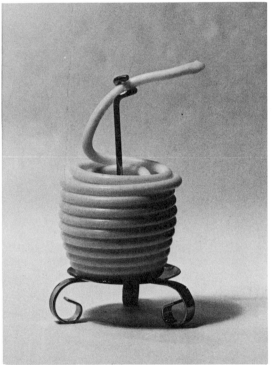

This modern-day version of the grandfather candle is made very much the same way as the ancient ones. Beeswax is melted in deep pots. Two people help pull the wick; at one end a person feeds it into the wax while the other person helps pull it out. When the wax hardens enough, it is wound into a form resembling a ball of thread.

This is a late eighteenth-century sterling silver candleholder and version of the grandfather candle from the area of Barcelona, Spain.

This eighteenth-century engraving shows beehives (Fig. 2), the press for extracting wax from honey (Fig. 7), vessels containing unrefined wax (Fig. 5).
Engraving from Duhamel du Monceau's book, 1762.

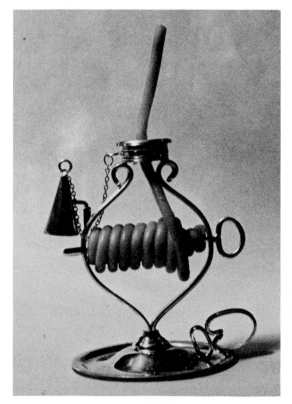

A contemporary version of the Spanish style of grandfather candle. Old versions of these candles can be traced to Turkey, Greece, and Spain.

This engraving from the eighteenth century shows an interior view of a wax foundry. The left wall consists of furnaces, and resting on their brickworks are caldrons (D) that are tin lined and equipped with spigots (G) from which hot wax is drawn off into containers. The tables (X) contain small wooden molds to hold beeswax. These cakes will be remelted later to make candles. *Engraving from Duhamel du Monceau's book, 1762.*

The candlemaker's entire family helps make these candles. Wax is melted in deep tin-coated copper pots and kept covered (otherwise wax turns green from the copper). Two people help pull the wick, one at one end to feed it into the wax and another to remove it. The wax is then left to harden. The wax ropes are wound like a ball of thread.

Through the Middle Ages the use of beeswax continued in importance. As mentioned earlier, wax was often taken in payment of tithes, and special beekeepers were appointed on large estates to take care of community needs. Wax manufacture gradually became a separate and important industry. Laws were enacted to keep the waxmakers honest. They had to stamp their sign on the wax, just in case it proved to be adulterated with cheaper tallow. By the time that Duhamel du Monceau wrote his remarkable book in 1762 on

the art of candle manufacture the production of candles had indeed reached a high. In fact, Campbell Morfit still considered Du Monceau's book a classic in 1847 because he almost literally copied its material for a section of his book. The nineteenth century did see much invention in candlemaking. If division of labor was a principle known to the wax industry it certainly was not practiced. The candlemaker not only prepared a special diet for his bees (six pounds of honey, one-quarter liter purée of lentils, white wine, and one fish, so that the beeswax would burn without odor or much smoke), he also separated the wax from the honey and purified the wax.

Variations in candle styles came about not entirely because of the whim and personality of craftsmen, but also because of the circumstances and environment in which people lived. For instance, early missionary priests

Eighteenth-century molds used for making wax and tallow candles. The methods for wicking, stringing, and typing operations are diagrammed here. Also note all the equipment used in order to fill a mold. *From Duhamel du Monceau's book, 1762.*

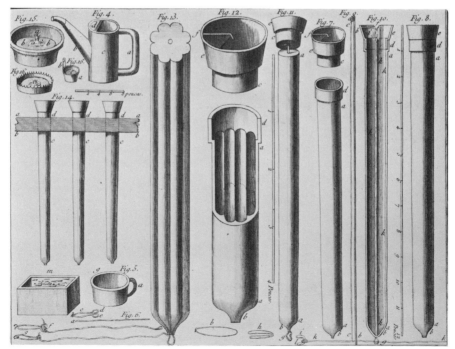

Pouring wax (or tallow) into molds did not change much after the eighteenth century. The candle craftsman today uses very similar methods. *From Duhamel du Monceau's book, 1762.*

who lived in the southwestern United States and Lower California used the wax covering of the boogum or cerio tree. Its waxy bark was peeled off; the wax was separated from the bark by boiling it in water and skimming the waxy residue off the top. It made a very fragrant type of altar candle and gave a clear, clean light, along with its built-in incense.

Bayberries were also used in much the same way by the settlers of Cape Cod. The custom of making bayberry candles still persists today. Besides being fragrant, they are ungreasy to the touch and their higher melting point gives them stiffness in hot weather.

Today, even the advent of sophisticated electric lighting systems has not made the candle obsolete. The candle still flatters with its glow on a woman's face; it still creates its own romantic atmosphere and radiates its warmth on special occasions.

Bayberry Candles

One and a half quarts of bayberries stripped from bushes in September make an 8″ taper. Cover the berries with water and boil them for five minutes. Work with small batches. After boiling, set the berries in a cool place until the wax rises to the top of the pot. Skim off the wax. Set this batch aside and repeat the operation until you have completed boiling all your berries.

Remelt the wax and let the impurities settle to the bottom. Strain this batch. Store the wax in tightly sealed cans until you are ready to make candles. The fragrance is fugitive and easily lost.

Dip or mold your candles and then store them in tightly sealed containers to maintain their fragrance.

The engraving depicts the candlemaking operation using the pouring method as it existed in France during the mid-eighteenth century. On the left, long *cierges* (church candles) are being formed and on the right bougies are being made. A ladle holding melted wax is emptied at the top of the candle pouring wax down the wick. The romaine, or hoop, is then rotated to the next candle. The hoop can be raised or lowered to accommodate different candle lengths by adjusting a pulley.

The candles are not completed in one operation; they are half finished and taken down from the ring, hung on hooks fastened to a board, and left to cool thoroughly. (If completed in one continual operation, the wax is likely to separate from the wick.) When finished, the candles are allowed to cool gradually between feathers and cloths (Fig. 15).

In Fig. 5 the workman, using a wooden planisher, revolves the candle (*cierge*) on a walnut table until it becomes even, smooth, and polished (d). Nearby the planisher is a vessel containing water so that the area can be dampened occasionally. *From Duhamel du Monceau's book, 1762.*

2

How to Make
a Structurally Sound Candle

PERIODICALS FIND CANDLEMAKING a popular subject because even the least skillful person can achieve a creditable result. These products are singularly attractive, but often the candle will not burn, will burn too fast, stay alight for a while and then smother in its wax or carbonaceous matter. Functioning candles, for example, cannot be successfully made with ordinary cord in place of wicking, or by using any old wax in any old way. There is a science to this age-old art. And although there are many approaches, general methods can be summarized from these many techniques.

What is a candle? We can define it many ways. There are the big flambeaux, or *cierges,* for church and ceremony, ornamental candles of sundry shapes and sizes, hurricane candles, votives—small, slow-burning night-lights—all

are usually made in molds. The other type belongs to the "dipping" class and consists mainly of tapers of varying sizes and those candles that are finished by dipping.

Structurally, a candle flame arises from a combustible, porous core, or wick, surrounded by the fuel, or flammable solid—the whole that makes up the candle. The candle flame is secured from three parts: the innermost nonluminous, gaseous section that consists of the liquid fuel melted by the heat and sucked up by capillary action along the wick and then vaporized by the heat; the second layer is vapor that is partly decomposed; and the third outside portion is where complete combustion takes place, yielding carbon dioxide and water vapor. A good burning candle requires the exact and correct proportion of

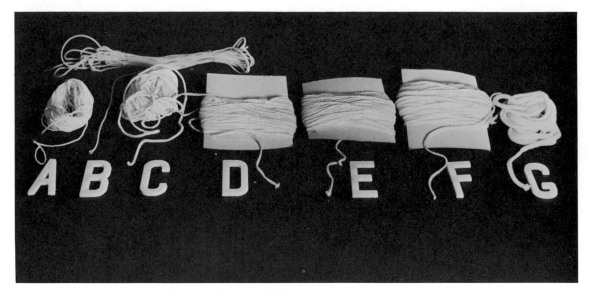

Various kinds of wicking:
    A. 12 thread unbleached flat braided
    B. wire wicking
    C. 18 thread bleached square braided *
    D. 24 thread bleached flat braided
    E. 30 thread bleached flat braided
    F. 36 thread bleached square braided
    G. 72 thread bleached square braided

fuel, heat, wick size, and treatment, and a spatial relation to each other. For example, if there is too much fuel or the wick too fat, then the flame will smother in melted wax; this is called guttering. The wax should not melt any faster than it can be sucked up the wick by capillary action, to be volatilized and burned. The size and construction of the wick, therefore, must be adjusted to the size and diameter of the candle and the melting point of the wax.

The Wick

When the candle is lighted and sucks up the liquefied fuel to be turned into vapor, the wick, if properly mordanted, becomes bent and the candle forms a cup shape at the wick's base. If the wick is not pickled (mordanted), it remains straight and a quantity of carbonaceous matter accumulates. As a result, the burning tip of the wick gives rise to a

smoky flame due to incomplete combustion. That is why there was once an occupation called candlesnuffer. These men went around with snuffing scissors, cutting off carbonaceous matter from wicks. When Cambacères invented the plaited wick in 1825, the candlesnuffer lost his job because the plaited wick dropped its tip outside the flame zone, and carbonaceous matter was dissipated automatically.

In a good burning candle, therefore, the tip of the wick bends *out* of the zone of combustion and is gradually reduced to a bead of glowing ash when the inorganic salts contained in the cellulose of the wick combine with the phosphates and borates of the mordanting salts and begin to glow in the hot flame. Then, being outside the flame zone, they automatically decompose. When the flame of the unplaited wick was extinguished, it would give off smoke and an odor of smoldering cellulose.

* Square braided wicks are less apt to curl and fall over when burning.

Contrasted with the loosely spun four to six strands of cotton for wicking used before 1825, the modern candlewick made of cotton yarn, ranging from four to nine and twenty to twenty-six in count, is plaited from three groups of yarn made up of three to twelve plaits per inch. This wick provides a two-inch flame with a three-eighth-inch diameter when installed in a candle made of paraffin and stearic acid with a one-inch diameter. Wick sizes are numbered according to the number of threads used. If thirty threads are used, then it is a thirty-ply wick.

Generally, the following holds true (variations of wax consistency and melting point cause slight differences):

Candle Diameter	Size of Wick
1" to 3"	15 ply
4" and tapers	24 ply
Over 4" and large tapers	30 ply

A wire wick, one that has meltable wire running up through the cotton wick, is used for night-lights—for slow burning, low-light-yield candles.

Today, the plaited wick is braided by machine and emerges as a flat, thin strip. Before chemical treatment, the plaited wick is boiled in weak caustic soda solution, bleached with chlorine or hypochlorite, scoured with hydrochloric acid, and washed with clear water—or may not be bleached at all. Excess water is centrifuged out and the mordanting solution is applied. Each producer has his own formula, though in the main the ingredients are ammonium phosphate, ammonium sulfate, ammonium chloride, borax, boric acid, and potassium nitrate.

One mordanting formula is:
7 grams ammonium phosphate
7 grams ammonium sulfate
0.5 grams borax
1,000 grams water

Mix together and either boil the wick in this solution for an hour, or soak for twenty-four hours. Usually, after pickling, the wicking is again centrifuged so that it will dry with an even salt coating. It is best to purchase the best wicking possible.

Wax

The primary components of present-day candles are paraffin and stearic acid. Paraffin emits a great deal of light for its weight, but the spread between its melting point and softening point is a drawback. Even a high-melting-point paraffin may be useful in hot weather, but in cold weather this wax takes longer to ignite and volatilize its fuel; therefore, because of insufficient paraffin, the candle dims out.

Stearine alone as candle wax cannot be used because of its crystalline nature—the mass crystallizes in its mold and cannot be removed. Also, the body of the candle is not

Various kinds of waxes used in candlemaking are shown here. Lower left are used beeswax candles; natural colored beeswax cakes are in the foreground. (They are in the same form as the eighteenth-century cakes. See engraving in Chapter 1.) To the right of the beeswax cakes is bleached beeswax and in the background are different melting point paraffins. Wax also can be purchased in prepared form for casting in metal molds, for sculpturing decorations; a foliating variety floats out of the candle sides forming a waxlike waterfall and lower melting point waxes for container candles such as glass. These waxes are balanced with various additives depending upon the purpose.

uniform throughout. Stearine would be effective if more than 5 percent paraffin is added, but it would be much too expensive. A combination of paraffin and stearic acid is ideal— a fully refined grade of paraffin with a melting-point range of 125°F. to 135°F. The stearic acid is sometimes called "double pressed" and is added in quantities of 5 to 30 percent; it imparts toughness to paraffin and greater wax density. The so-called nondrip candle is made by dipping candles into mixtures containing higher and higher percentages of stearic acid. The first dips are in a mixture of 5 to 10 percent stearic acid, and after two-thirds of the candle body is completed, the final mixture contains 20 to 30 percent stearic acid. When this candle burns, the inner core melts more rapidly than the outer layer, thus forming a cup to hold the fluid fuel until it is absorbed by its wick. This cup keeps the paraffin from dripping down the sides of the candle.

Some candle wax formulas are:

70% paraffin	or 90% paraffin	for church candles
20% stearic acid	10% stearic acid	48% paraffin
10% beeswax		52% beeswax

The temperature of your wax should be taken before pouring.

Five percent candelilla, or 3 percent carnuba, can be added to raise the melting point of the candle wax. Note that if wax has light blemishes or spots under its surface, it is because the wax has been reheated too often; it breaks down.

Melting Wax

The traditional way of melting wax with safety is to melt the wax in the top section of a double boiler or to use an electric crock or frying pan where the electric elements are unexposed.

Most waxes melt at a temperature range between 110°F. and 200°F. The boiling point of water is 213°F. Spattering of wax occurs when water hits hot wax when wax is *above* the boiling point of water. At this point an explosive reaction can result. Wax does not have a boiling point, except for chemical purposes where it occurs at 600°F. to 700°F. under a vacuum. Its relatively high flash point of 400°F. is the point at which flame will ignite vapors. (A material such as benzine has a flash point of 12°F., turpentine 95°F.) The National Board of Fire Underwriters places liquids that have flash points above 70°F. in

Hardening materials for paraffin-beeswax candles are:
A. Unpressed stearic acid
B. Triple pressed stearic acid
C. Luster crystals that are really a polyethylene type of pellet or Elvax.

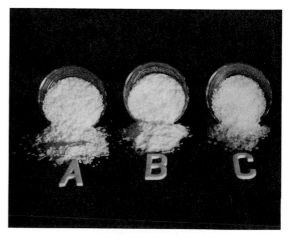

SOLVENTS FOR WAX AND MELTING POINT RANGE

KIND OF WAX	MELTING POINT RANGE	ORIGIN	SOLUBILITY
Bayberry	113° F.–114.8° F.	vegetable	alcohol
Beeswax (natural)	144° F.–147° F.	insect	ether, chloroform, benzene, carbon disulfide
Beeswax (bleached)	144° F.–147° F.	insect	ether, chloroform, benzene
Candelilla	154° F.–158° F.	vegetable	carbon tetrachloride, turpentine
Paraffin	118° F.–165° F.	mineral	benzene, chloroform, carbon disulfide, turpentine
Stearic Acid	131° F. second modification 161° F.	synthetic	partially in alcohol, ether

Trichloroethane (vinyl trichloride) and Triasol (trichlorethylene and ethylene dichloride) are used as wax solvents and to clean wax from molds.

Class III, the safest category. If wax is melted directly over a flame, however, the fire can leap up the sides of the pot, particularly if wax is allowed to remain on the sides of the pot, and ignite the liquid wax. There are several ways to solve this hazard. Use a double boiler, using the top of the pot for the wax and heating water in the bottom section. This way wax can never exceed the boiling point of water. Or melt wax in a heating container that does not have exposed heating elements, such as an electric frying pan, or a crock pot. Incidentally, never leave wax unattended if you are using exposed flames or exposed elements. A pot can spring a leak and the weld in a can can melt. Also, do not pour or cast near an open flame. Keep powdered baking soda nearby to extinguish flames. NEVER use water!

Coloring for Wax Candles

Waxy crayons, dyes such as Tintex and Rit, and powder paints have been recommended for coloring wax. These, however, leave residue and color unevenly. Crayons cause a chemical reaction that "eats up" the wick and can put out the candle. Oil colors, for painting, also have been employed as a colorant for hot wax, but are expensive and difficult to mix evenly. The best kind of oil color is supplied by color manufacturers for high temperature applications. Candle manufacturers use an oil-soluble aniline dye. These colors have to withstand heat, light, and the acid nature of stearic acid. In any case, the amount of color used can vary between 0.05 or 0.01 percent by the weight of the amount of stearic acid used and the depth

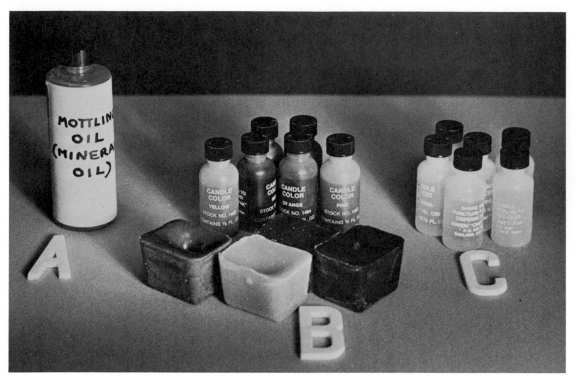

Various additives used in making a candle. A. Mineral oil, 3 percent will mottle a candle. B. Two forms of candle color are shown here—liquid and cake; powdered color is used by professionals who mix large batches of color. C. Candle scent, oil-based. Scents are rated by the percentage needed to scent a pound of wax. The higher the percentage rating the weaker the scent—and the more needed to scent a pound of wax. For example, a scent rated 4 percent will require four times as much scent per pound as a scent rated 1 percent.

of color desired. If there is no stearic acid used in the wax formula, then substitute oil colorants. The pigments would probably be more stable. Never use a water-based color, or food color. Remember too, most wax color gets lighter as it hardens. Make adjustment in mixing your colors. For professional candles that must stand up to actinic light rays that discolor aniline dyes, add 0.05 percent Tinuvin P, an ultraviolet light absorber (Geigy Industrial Chemicals, Ardsley, New York). It not only minimizes fading but also aids in the thermal stability of some wax soluble dyes that change due to the heat of the wax.

Novelty Color Effects

Novelty sometimes dictates varicolored candlelight. Candle flame can vary in hue depending upon what chemicals are added to the wax:

Sodium chlorate or potassium nitrate makes yellow;
Strontium nitrate makes red;
Calcium chloride makes orange;
Borax, copper nitrates, barium nitrate make green;
Copper chloride makes blue green;
Lithium chlorate makes purple.

These chemicals can either be added to the wax, or the wick can be soaked in the chemical solution for a time.

Perfuming the Wax

Candle wax can be scented to give off an aroma when burning, with an oil-based scent or a perfume with an oil base. Oil is the only compatible base for a wax candle. Oils like sandalwood, patchouli, vetiver, and kewda are sometimes used for exotic effects. There are virtually hundreds of scents available.

The best way to perfume your wax is to add the scent to the melted wax just prior to pouring the mold. A quarter of an ounce of pure *undiluted* oil scent is enough to perfume two to three pounds of wax. Other methods used are to saturate your wick in candle scent before attaching it to your mold; or to add the same amount of scent for a whole candle to the amount of wax you use to fill the well, or cavity, that forms around the wick as the candle cools. Take care not to use an excessive amount of perfume oil to the wax prior to pouring wax into your mold, else the oil could cause mottling—then again, you may want this effect.

Additives such as mineral oil, color, scents are added to the wax just before pouring.

Casting or Molding

Basic candlemaking methods are dipping, pouring, and casting or molding—the latter is probably the most popular because of its great variety and design possibilities. Generally, for pouring, a mold container is used. It can be almost anything from pewter to tin, glass, plaster, epoxy, rubber—anything that will allow the release of the wax candle and will not melt under the heat of the melted wax; and allow wick lengths to be fastened in some way so that they can be centered and kept vertical—two more essentials for a good burning candle.

Another requisite, one that is really critical, is the temperature of the wax for pouring. Wax should be hot enough to flow evenly, but not so hot that it drains excessively. Thermometer testing is recommended. Casting should be on the high side of the wax's

Commercial types of molds for candlemaking made of ceramic, polyethylene, glass, aluminum, and tin.

These are just a few of many different kinds of possible molds one finds around the house.

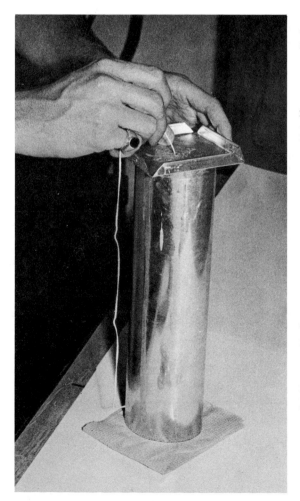

(a) Stringing of a mold is accomplished by threading wicking in the hole at the base of your mold,

melting point, unless you have to weld one pouring to another; in that case the heat can be higher. Two hundred and ten degrees F. is an average maximum. If a frosted result is obtained, then the casting temperature was too low. If the wax is too hot, it may be very difficult to remove the candle from its mold. And if the candle is cooled too rapidly, air holes and bubbles will form in the wax. These air holes and bubbles can also lead to candle cave-ins, excessive dripping, and rapid burning caused by excess air in the candle fuel.

Many of the popular "how-to" articles on candlemaking show use of milk cartons for molding. They have to be used with care because if the melting point of the wax is higher than the polyethylene-wax coating on the milk carton, the container will collapse and hot wax will pour out of its seams. Most of the time, wax of a lower-than-carton-wax temperature has to be used, therefore producing a dull-finished product. But if the candle is to be coated in some way afterward, the quality of the undersurface does not matter.

(b) Tying the wick at the hole and attaching it with putty or very sticky adhesive tape,

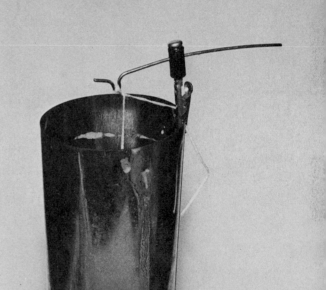

(c) An alligator clip can be used to hold the wick taut and in place in the center of the mold.

Spraying a mold with silicone spray. Take care not to inhale the spray.

PRIMER OF CHEMICAL CANDLE ADDITIVES

ADDITIVE	RESULT
Cetyl Alcohol	makes wax softer, more malleable, increases size of flame
Elvax 310, 350, 360 (150° F., 10% Elvax) ethylene/vinylacetate copolymer	makes wax tough, flexible, adhesive, superior gloss retention
Polyethylene	makes wax harder and glossier, carvable
Stearic Acid	makes wax harder
Venice Turpentine	makes wax more flexible and adhesive

Types of Molds

Here are some of the most popular materials used for various types of molds:

> cardboard tubes, cartons, corrugated forms
> cheap glassware, old bottles that can be broken and removed
> plaster
> various plastics, including epoxy and RTV types
> aluminum, all shapes and sizes without undercuts
> pewter
> cast iron
> earthenware
> eggshells
> flexible rubber
> wood, sand, clay
> tin, including tin cans
> gelatin

Separators for Molds

Most mold materials have to be coated with oil or silicone to ensure easy separation of the wax candle from the mold. Just swab a very, very thin film of oil on the mold surface; excess oil will cause air bubbles to form. Peanut oil is a good material. A thin layer of silicone spray will work beautifully too. Wipe out excess. If plaster is used, soak the mold in warm water. The plaster should be thoroughly wet but not dripping excess moisture. Soaping with a green soap or Ivory soap comes next, before pouring the hot wax into the cavity.

When using glass with undercutting, making it impossible to pull out the candle, or when utilizing any glass, such as bottles, score the glass bottle with a glass cutter. Wrap it in a heavy cloth, strike the scored line with a hammer, refrigerate the bottle overnight, or soak it in ice-cube water, and rewrap the bottle in cloth, or in a plastic bag, and plunge it into very hot water again. As soon as you hear the glass crack remove it from the water, before the wax has a chance to remelt, and carefully lift the cracked glass from the wax.

Special techniques of working with the wax will be dealt with as various candle styles are discussed.

Inserting the Wicking

When the mold has been prepared, set it aside and get the wicking ready while the wax is melting. A candle may be cast with or without wicking. In the former, some method has to be worked out so that the wick is in the exact center of the wax form and is vertically taut besides. One solution, using cardboard material, is to tie a slipknot into the plaited wick and thread it through a hole in the bottom center of the container. Draw it tightly so that the slipknot plugs up

This candle was made only with paraffin in a milk carton (note the dull bubbly surface). A heated ice pick is used to make a hole to accommodate the wick. *Courtesy Gulf Oil Corp.*

An electric drill may also be used to pierce a hole into a wax form. *Courtesy Gulf Oil Corp.*

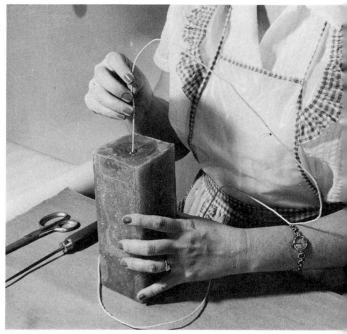

A wick stiffened with wax is strung through the hole. This candle will either have to be dipped into hot wax or decorated in order to cover the surface imperfections. *Courtesy Gulf Oil Corp.*

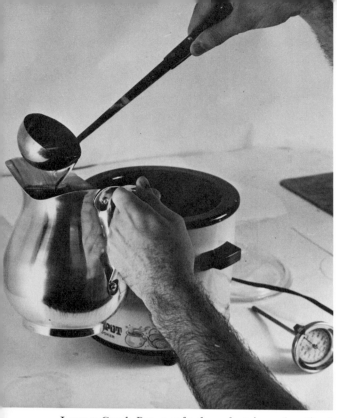

I use a Crock Pot, a safe slow electric cooker lined with stoneware to melt wax. At times I have kept wax melted for twenty-four hours. The cooker has two speeds—low and high—and uses only fifty watts. Wax is ladled from the cooker into a seamless aluminum pitcher that has a dripless pouring edge.

Wax Measurement

To determine how much wax to use in order to fill a mold, measure the quantity first by filling the mold container with water. Then draw the comparison—the water will approximate how much wax you will need. Pour the water into the pot you are to use to melt the wax. Draw a line on the pot to indicate the level. Then make an adjustment by estimating that wax expands when heated. A four-ounce solid chunk of wax will measure five ounces when heated. And the wax will contract commensurately when cooled, particularly in the last area that cools, the core or center. (A natural pit or depression will be left because of this.) Be certain to dry the pot thoroughly before melting the wax.

Pouring the Wax

When pouring the wax, start with a small amount in the bottom; when it sets up, pour the rest, at a hotter temperature than at first. This method is particularly important when wicking is attached to the base and when the

Floss Perisho pouring into a gang of molds. Her granddaughter is watching and learning.

the carton hole and reinforce with sticky adhesive tape or a glob of putty used in glazing windows; cut V shapes on the top of the carton sidewalls, and with a stick or match held across the carton's opening and resting in the notches, attach the wicking to the center of this horizontal brace; or let the wick hang loosely on the side and fasten it tightly with a rubber band around the carton anchoring the wick.

If no wicking is to be used, then a heated ice pick or knitting needle can puncture a hole in the wax and then wicking, stiffened with wax, can be strung through. An electric drill can also be used to drill a hole—in some cases it may be more expedient.

Now that the mold is coated, and the wick is in place, the mold is ready to receive the melted wax.

mold base has a seam. After the wax has been poured to the top of the mold and it cools, a scum or crust will form on the top surface. Puncture that layer with a stick or pencil down into the gelatinous mass the full length of the candle. This "opens" the candle, eliminates air pockets, and ensures more even burning. Refill the contraction depressions with more wax two or three times as the mass cools. Do not be too hasty to strip or remove the candle from its mold.

ANOTHER SOUND
CANDLE WAX FORMULA

10 lbs. paraffin 133° F. melting point
 1 lb. stearic acid
        triple pressed (all impurities are removed in triple pressed stearic acid)
½ lb. beeswax
Courtesy Emily McGowan, The Candle Farm

Cooling and Removal from the Mold

Some professionals recommend cooling their molded candles initially in a water bath in order to obtain a glossy finish. I do not find this necessary. If you wish to try this technique, find a container that is deep enough to hold your mold. A wastepaper basket, garbage pail, or restaurant-type-size vegetable can will do. After filling your mold with wax, allow it to settle for a few seconds. Gently tap the sides to release air bubbles that may stick to the mold, then immerse the mold in a lukewarm water bath to within one inch of the top of your mold (enough for you to grip the top of your mold). Take care not to get water into your wax. Then weigh down the mold by placing a heavy object over the mold. Do not keep the mold in the water bath for more than two hours. Every forty-five minutes or so, you can refill the cavity that forms around the wick, while the candle mold is sitting in its water bath.

Cooling can also be speeded up by refrigerating the mold and rotating it every half hour while in the refrigerator so that one side does not cool more quickly than another. Remove the mold from the refrigerator as soon as the mold material, the surface, feels cool. If (thermal) cracks form in the candle's surface, it is because the refrigerator was too cold, or the candle was left in the refrigerator too long.

Allow the wax to cool *completely* before taking it from the mold. Sometimes it may take eight to twenty-four hours, depending upon the size of the candle. After the candle comes out of the mold, let it hang or cure for

four or more days; it will be stronger then, because the molecules have to reorient themselves. Before the candles are left to age, however, remove excess wax and imperfections from seams, if there are any, and from the top outer edge, with a warm, sharp tool. This is sometimes called "butting."

After the candle has cooled for at least eight hours, turn the mold upside down and tap it gently on a hard surface. The candle should slide out easily. If it does not, then refrigerate it for about an hour and try again. If you still have difficulty, then your last resort is to run hot water over the mold surface. This softens the wax and can ruin your candle, but the candle will come out of the mold. (Later on you can dip this candle in hot wax to form a coating that will repair the surface.) Never beat or pry the candle from the mold because indentations caused by beating and scratches resulting from prying will make subsequent candles difficult to remove and you will do irreparable damage to the candle as well.

After the candle has aged, if frost patches appear, perhaps because of a low casting temperature, remove these imperfections by rubbing the wax with carbon tetrachloride. For a high sheen, you can dip the whole candle into a tall container of melted wax and then, in a few seconds, into cool water. Or buff the candle with a soft, lintless, dampened cloth, or rub with a nylon stocking. Another method of polishing is to moisten a soft woolen cloth with ammoniated alcohol and polish the candle to a high shine. Sometimes candles are dipped into lacquer to give

This early eighteenth-century New England revolving candle dipping stand was a standard piece of furniture in colonial times. *Courtesy The Metropolitan Museum of Art*

them a high gloss as well. This is popular in southern Europe and Asia Minor. Polyvinyl acetate/chloride or a product called Mod-Podge also can be used as a glaze.

Dipping and Pouring

The second most important candle-forming method, dipping and pouring, was perhaps the earliest technique in candlemaking. The method used to make these candles today is much the same as the ancient craft or the dipping bees of Colonial days. Of course, mechanical devices have greatly increased commercial candle production, but handcraft in making tapers, for instance, is still very much the same.

In the pouring method, wicking, weighted at the end to keep it taut, is suspended, usu-

ally from a wire hoop, like a wagon wheel (romaine), and hot wax is poured from a pitcher over the wicking in successive layers— with cooling and aging stages. And finally, the tapers are rolled to a hard, smooth texture. Or, in dipping, a single wick or wicking wound around a rectangular iron form is successively dipped into a vat containing hot wax. After the proper number of dippings, cooling, and hardening in sequence, the candles are cut loose and trimmed. This operation is more skilled than it sounds because the temperature of the wax bath is critical. Too hot a melt will disolve wax layers, too cool a fluid will congeal unevenly. If the candles air cool, they obtain a satinlike finish; and if they are machine polished with felt buffs or rolled on a glass table, they emerge with a gloss.

George Arnold, candlemaker, demonstrating candle dipping at a Pennsylvania fair.

A simple version of the pouring method—good for making one or two candles—hot wax of 165° F. is poured down a piece of wicking until there is enough of a wax buildup. Care should be taken to allow the previously poured wax to cool somewhat before pouring the next layer so that the new hot wax does not continually melt away previous pourings.

After the wax has cooled for about twenty minutes, roll out the candle on a warm glass sheet to even out the texture. This step is optional. Then allow the candle to hang undisturbed for twenty-four hours so that the wax molecules can orient themselves.

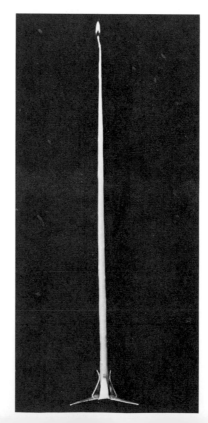

This thin taper is 18" long and still has the slightly irregular qualities of a hand poured candle.

MAKING THE BASIC CANDLE

Gather together all your materials for making a basic candle: melting container, wax, stearic acid, wicking, and beeswax, if you plan to use beeswax; plus additives such as color, scent; along with your mold, mold release agent, wax-pouring pitcher, thermometer, scissors, and putty, to complete the array.

According to your formula, weigh your paraffin wax until you are familiar enough with proportions to mix ingredients like "grandma the cook." Weights and measures are usually not so critical and precise in candlemaking as they are in other fields using chemical materials. The formula used for this candle was 90 percent paraffin and 10 percent stearic acid. Other formulas work as well, depending upon the purpose and function of the candle. Church candles are practically all beeswax. Slow burning, very hard, opaque candles are made up almost entirely of stearic acid. When estimating the amount of wax you will need, follow the wax measurement estimating procedures described in the text.

Weigh your stearic acid. Ten percent is weighed here, taking into account an adjustment in weight for the paper cup.

While the wax is melting, add your measured amount of stearic acid. Place the lid on this type of container and melt the stearic acid together wtih your wax.

You can prepare your mold or molds while the wax is melting. Select your mold; make certain it is clean. Spray or coat your mold with a mold release. Silicone is being used in this case.

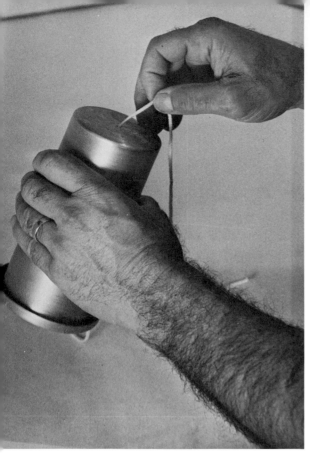

Thread your wicking into the hole that is in the base of your mold. Make certain that the proper size and type of wick is used. Selection of wicking depends upon the purpose of your candle and the type of wax used as well as the size of your candle. Guidelines are given in the text.

Knot the end of your wicking so that it does not slip through the mold wicking hole. Be generous and allow an extra amount of wicking to extend beyond the mold container's length, so that the wicking can be supported and centered.

Seal the mold hole and wicking knot with a plastic putty such as Mortite. Some chandlers use duck tape or a very sticky adhesive tape. It does not matter what you use, so long as the mold does not leak and the sealer is removable.

With a small amount of tension, wrap the wicking around a stick or a wick bar until the wick is taut and centered. Tape the end of the wick to your mold to ensure no slippage. This mold has no phlange at the base; therefore, in order for the mold to stand in a level, upright position, it is placed on a small can, otherwise the knot and putty at the base would not permit the mold to stand straight.

Then, after the wax has melted, ladle or pour the mixture into a warmed pitcher for pouring. The wax at this point will probably be above pouring temperature. An average wax pouring temperature of about 165° F. was used here, but this can vary. Wax coming directly from your crock pot or frying pan could be 185° F. or higher, and wax melted in the top of a double boiler will be about 213° F. if left to heat long enough.

Attach your temperature gauge to your pitcher to ascertain the most propitious pouring temperature for your wax formula. Then add your additives, such as coloring. The colorant used here is especially prepared for candlemakers and is intense color already mixed into wax and poured into ice cube sized pieces. Merely scrape off the amount of color you would like. Colors can be mixed according to the most personal and subtle hues, values, and intensities.

If you choose to scent your candle, now is the time to add your oil-based perfume. And if you wish a mottled surface, add your mineral oil now. It works best if you use a pure paraffin candle formula.

When the wax temperature reaches the proper point you are ready to pour your wax. Pour a small amount of wax to seal the hole at the base of your mold. Allow it to set up before slowly filling the entire mold container. When pouring, aim for the center of the mold so that the hot wax, as it is poured, carries up the bubbles to the surface instead of trapping them, and so that the wax that is being poured does not wash down into the wax mold release. Save some wax for later use in filling a cavity in the candle.

After the candle has hardened, for about an hour, depending upon climatic conditions and your cooling method (room temperature conditions of about 72° F. were present here), pierce the top hardened layer of wax with a knife or stick the full length of your candle, if necessary.

You will discover that there is a hole in your candle that extends most of the way down along your wick. This is caused by the congealing and contraction of wax along the fastest cooling areas of your mold, causing the wax molecules to contract toward the mold surfaces.

Refill the hole to the top with more wax and allow it to congeal.

Pierce the top of the mold again, if necessary, and refill the cavity with wax. You may have to repeat the operation two or three more times until the candle is a solid wax form. Unless the candle is solid wax, it will not burn properly.

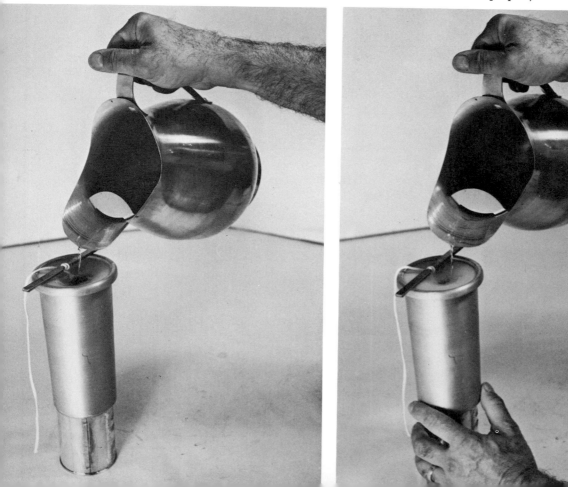

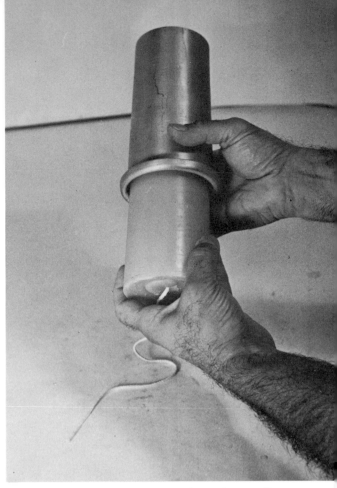

Do not be too hasty to remove the candle from the mold. Wait at least eight hours. Then remove the plastic putty and unknot the wick.

Tap the mold gently on its sides. The candle should slide out easily. If it does not, observe the precautions and methods described in the text.

Clip off excess wicking. The top of the mold now becomes the base of the candle.

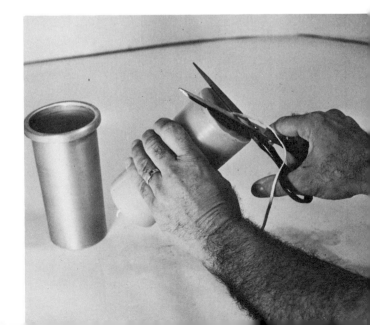

35

Scrape away excessive wax, as in the edging (caused by the capillary action of wax rising above its surface onto the mold material), or as mold seams. This mold is a continuous spun aluminum tube and has no seams.

Because wax duplicates the interior surface of your mold material, you may find, as with a spun aluminum surface, that your wax surface requires some polishing. A nylon stocking with *nothing* on it works splendidly.

The resulting candle is sound. It burns well. I used this as a base candle for almost all the candles used in Chapter 4. Note that the wicking is still a bit too long for burning, but provides, at this point, a great anchor for dipping and other finishing techniques.

Candle Clinic

PROBLEM	POSSIBLE CAUSES	SOLUTIONS
Surface Problems		
Candle Surface Soiled	exposed to environment too long; excessively handled	rub candle with soft rag saturated with cooking oil or baby oil; let stand about 15 minutes, then gently buff; scrape candle with dull knife and then redip at 220°F.
Fractures and Cracks	candle contact with cold too soon or for too long caused thermal stresses	even when rushed, reduce amount of time candle spends in cold water, refrigerator, or freezer
Frost Marks	excessive adhesion to sides of mold	try using hotter wax (over 180°F.); try warming mold before casting
Dull Surface	mold has dull surface; or a wax carton coated with a low melting point wax was used	polish candle with a nylon stocking; polish with cooking oil or baby oil; spray with p.v.a.; coat with Mod-Podge; redip in wax at 220°F.
Blisters and Pimples	storage in too warm a place causes air in candle to expand and combine into bubbles	store candles in cooler location; scrape candle with dull knife and redip in wax at 220°F.
Spots Under Surface	wax has been reheated too often and has broken down	use fresh wax; redip candle at 220°F. or decorate to mask imperfections
Pit Marks	too fast filling of mold causes turbulence that traps air bubbles along mold wall; dust in mold	slow up filling; clean mold before filling
Soft White Mottling	too much oil on surface of mold (can deliberately create this effect with 3% mineral oil mixed into molten wax); wax cools too slowly allowing large crystals to form near walls of mold	reduce amount of oil used as mold release; speed up cooling of mold; cut down on the amount of scent used
Lines of Tiny Bubbles Ring the Candle	hot water bath too turbulent; water for water bath added after candle was placed in mold	slow up insertion and withdrawal of candle from water bath; eliminate this technique and use wax dipping method

PROBLEM	POSSIBLE CAUSES	SOLUTIONS
Mold Problems		
Candle Will Not Release	wick still attached to base of mold; no mold release used; mold is scratched or dented; wax is too soft; wax cools too slowly; under-cuts in mold	drop mold onto a soft pad; release wick; use mold release; place mold in refrigerator for a few minutes; buy or make a new mold
Candle Bulges at Sides	usually when cardboard carton is used as mold	support sides of container with stiff cardboard, masonite, or wood and attach with string (rubber bands may buckle carton); scrape away excess and decorate or redip
Cave-in on Sides	candle well was not pierced early enough; cavity in center of candle caused walls to contract inward	poke a hole in the well before wax begins to harden; use candle as base for thick types of decorations
Glass Molds Will Not Break	glass too thick; no mold release used in mold; wax that is too soft tends to stick to the glass	refrigerate candle for 8 hours and then immediately submerge it in boiling water; remove with care immediately
Wax Chips at Base	when candle is turned so that well becomes the base, the well may have been filled too high and its wax not hot enough to adhere to the "old" wax on the surface; wax was too hard; mold refrigerated too long results in thermal shock and chipping	don't fill well to overflowing; reduce amount of hardeners used such as stearic acid; cut down cooling time
Candle-Burning Problems		
Excessive Smoking	wick is too large and flame consumes wax faster than wick can absorb melted wax; candle in draft	reduce size of wick

PROBLEM	POSSIBLE CAUSES	SOLUTIONS
Excessive Dripping	wick is too small and cannot absorb the amount of wax melted, therefore melted wax overflows; candle in draft and melted wax is "blown" over edge; wax that is too soft (or has a low melting point) will melt too rapidly for the wick to absorb it and will overflow	enlarge size of wick; keep away from drafts; add stearic acid to wax
Splattering	air in cavities left in candle expands due to heat of flame causing flame to burst forth bringing bits of molten wax with it	pierce well around wick, fill cavity more than once if necessary
Rapid Burning	excess air in the fuel because candle is cooled too rapidly will cause the wick flame to burn higher and faster	slow down cooling process; use higher melting point wax; add stearic acid; pour more slowly

Candle Designing

Types of Candles and Decoration

A CANDLE IS A light source that dramatizes its environment as it burns. Its shape is usually a pillar or a column that can be seen from all sides. Whether the candle is consumed in the burning process or whether it burns leaving an external shell that later can be replenished, its form should suit its purpose.

If the candle is to consume itself, then decoration should be very simple. It would be ugly if candle drippings poured over the design, or if parts of a form, like a head or arm, were consumed leaving the incomplete remainder of a sculptured form. The shape of this type of candle can have tremendous variety. Some may be very thin, others short and chunky, still others may be shaped as triangles, or curved and spiraled.

Those candles that provide a predominantly decorative function for special occasions or permanent arrangements permit a variety of decorative surfaces, and so can the candle that leaves a shell as it burns.

In all cases, for all types, a candle is meant to burn and not to sit in its holder forever waiting to function as a candle. A candle that is never burned is a static form. But when lighted, a candle is capable of transforming the atmosphere into a living place. Flickering of light creates everchanging transformations of the environment with a warm ambience, with mysteries in its shadows and flattery in its brightness.

The Candle as Wax

Contemporary candles are made of waxes,

different combinations and proportions certainly, but intrinsically candles are wax. And wax has qualities that need to be considered when designing a candle. Wax can be pressed, rolled, shaped, cut, colored, glued, pulled, melted, poured, carved, painted, and molded. Wax is not paper, wood, metal, or fabric and, therefore, should not be treated as another material or be made to imitate a foreign texture.

Candles That Defy Good Design Principles

There are some candles that are atrocious because they violate all elements of good design. Generally, these candles impose on the candle something that it is not. For example, a candle is not a statue, or a sculpture with a wick. A candle is not a greeting card with a message glued to its surface. A candle is not an iced cake, or wood, or metal. Wax should look like what it is, and its surface should represent what wax will do when treated in various ways.

Exceptions

Whenever possible, decorations should be an integral part of the surface and not a superficial aspect, unless the decorations used relate to the candle in addition to another function, such as a flower arrangement around the base of the candle. Decorations should not impede the burning of the candle, catch fire, or be buried in wax drippings as the candle burns.

There are other exceptions. The "Pop" candle, for instance, is a class of candle that challenges the meaning of the candle as a good design form, sacrificing good design for the sake of humor. The "Crayola" crayon candle pokes fun at the idea of a wax crayon by exaggerating its size and giving the crayon another purpose. This particular candle—an enlarged wax crayon—becomes something it is not, but, on the other hand, almost is. It is funny. The lemon meringue pie slice that looks good enough to eat, but lights up instead, is humorous as a pop form, but comes very close to being a display model for a restaurant. It must be considered that the pop candle is a fad form—but each candle has a temporary life anyway. Pop art is a twentieth-century phenomenon, but the candle form existed as long as the world had civilization. This marraige of tradition with newness can be refreshingly funny.

Evaluating Good and Bad Design

Candles can be proportioned well or uninterestingly—extreme sizes often are more satisfying visually than forms having equal depth, height, and width. The tall thin candle and the extremely flat squat candle are more attractive than a square shape. But variations in form can become *too much* by incorporating too many "good" things all in the same candle. Restraint is the answer. Try to control decorations on shapes by including those decorations that look like parts of the candle. Do decorate the candle that has a basic geometric shape, but don't impose decoration on the candle if the candle is very unusual in shape, or if the candleholder is very important and attracts attention. For example, elaborate silver or wrought iron candelabras should contain very simple candle shapes.

The Candleholder

Let us review. Candles should stand upright (except for the long super-thin tapers) and not droop or drip to one side. The candle usually is a pillar or column that should be seen from the front as well as all around. The candleholder is for holding the candle, so that the candle does not fall or drip wax onto the table. Its base can either hug the candle in its hollow, hold the candle through a pressure device, or fix the candle with a pin that pierces the candle underneath its base.

Because the candleholder for consumable candles has to have some kind of a bobeche shape (a saucerlike form encircling the candle) to catch possible melted wax, consideration should be given to the size of the saucer

This imitation onyx Chinese-style candle has a very pleasing translucent surface. Wax can be a clever imitator. But when this candle burns its form will be a fraction of a sculpture and not a very pretty candle.

This wax sculpture candle, inspired by an African wood carving, is bad design because it pretends to be what it is not—a wood carving. After the horns (candles) are lighted the form is fragmented into a partial shape.

What is this form: a box, a vase? Note by the flame that it is a candle. Because of its metallic finish it does not have the appearance of a wax candle even though the proportion and texture is otherwise very attractive.

A slice of lemon meringue that looks good enough to eat, but burns instead, defies good design by becoming good humor.

These eggs burn to reveal yellow yolks—another pop art addition to candlemaker's wit.

Chocolate scented candle kisses and a wax scented wax candle crayon play on humor and become candles as entertainment.

A book of matches enlarged twenty times with matches that burn—why not?

A bulb that gives off light and screws into a real socket can become an electric bulb for an electricless camping site.

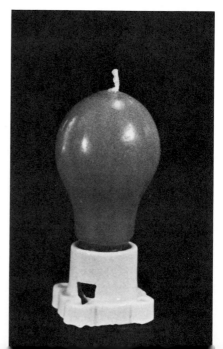

These candleholder designs range from traditional to modern—from England to Denmark, Israel, Japan, and America. Some are machine-made, some handmade, but all contain a hole into which the candle fits. All flair out beneath the hole to catch dripping wax.

These candleholders hearken back to past oriental tradition, when candlewicks were made of rolled paper or reed shapes that fit over pins. The pin is an efficient way of keeping a candle in place. The large saucer shape on the left is weighted to support large or tall candles.

The two varieties of candleholders on the left are tension types that spring snugly onto the candles to hold them in place. The candleholder second from the right is a saucer type that supports block-type candles. And the candleholder on the right is multipurposed —it can hold tapers in its holes or support various types of curved forms.

in proportion to the base and the candle size. In some way, the base also needs to be weighted in order to balance tall or large candles. Candleholders may be designed to stay in one location, to be attached to a wall or ceiling, or to be transportable. If movable, the holder should have some kind of handle or stem and a somewhat larger saucer or bobeche to catch wax drippings as moving air fans the flame.

Styles

Since candles were requirements for lighting in the past, the candleholder has reflected a variety of styles. In fact, the twentieth century has seen excellent new design solutions for candleholders. Each age has developed its own answers for candleholder forms. Even today, possibilities for new designs in candles and candleholders seem almost limitless. Whereas in the past each object emerged through trial and error developing with small changes, today our scientific-technological knowledge, as well as our broad range of information about other societies, has enabled us to produce original shapes that combine precision and economy as well as beauty in candle forms for contemporary environments. Since the candle now, for most people, is not a necessity, but rather an embellishment to make the quality of life more pleasant, candle shapes and their holders have emerged to complement the home environment. This does not mean that the modern room should be swamped by candle objects, but points more clearly to basic shapes with their intrinsic patterns. Simple shapes are efficient and honest no less today than yesterday.

It should be obvious that the candleholder on the right is more attractive and appropriate for the shape and size of this candle. The form of this candle, by the way, hearkens back to an ancient Chinese form. A hole in its base, if it were an old oriental original, would have been formed of a rolled paper wick and would, as this one, fit on a spiked base.

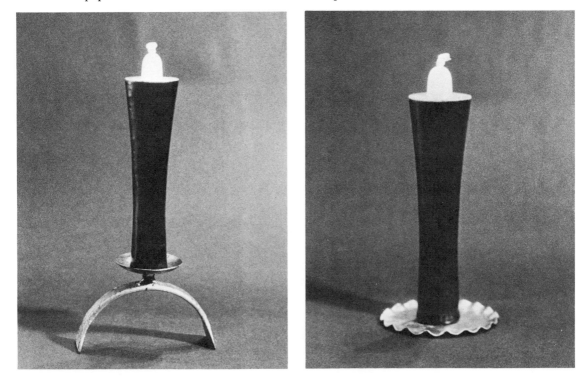

Grouping of these very thin tapers can create a very pleasing pattern of diagonals and shadows. The wrought-iron candleholder has enough weight to hold these candles in position adequately.

Both of these wax candle forms are "cute"—and somewhat funny. As the owl burns down the sand-wax body will become a container candle. The other candle is an imaginary creature anyway so it does not matter what shape the form will take when burning.

A Primer of Good Design Techniques

Inspiration for beautiful candles comes from a variety of sources. Sometimes something you may see, such as a rock or a pinecone, can inspire a design idea. Other times designs evolve with modification from other candle forms that have been made. Copying someone else's idea does not lead to anything but short-range technical satisfaction. To maintain the challenge of candlemaking over a long period of time is to invent, to improvise, and to discover new ways of working and new ways of seeing wax as a material. Design ideas can also spring from other sectors such as exploring form, surface, use of color, and organization of these aspects into different combinations.

Form

We see three-dimensional forms not only as a whole, but by contour. What kind of outline does the candle form make? How does the contour or outline relate to the decorations?

Do your candle forms have a feeling of mass or do they appear fragile? How does the candle as a solid relate to its purpose—decoration, use? How does the candle mass relate to the candleholder?

Candle forms usually are symmetrical, but it is possible to design a candle form that is not the same shape on all sides. What would happen if you started with a basic form idea and then mentally stretched the shape, compressed it, twisted it, or bent it?

Look at unrelated objects and see whether you can adapt an element of that shape to your idea. For example, the shape of a cattail plant, the dial of a telephone, a stamper (the kind used with a stamp pad) turned upside down, a chair leg, a fork, and so on.

Surface

The outer face or exterior of the candle can have countless variations. Look at the texture of the wax. Is is coarse and chunky in appearance or is it fine and smooth? Does the surface have a matte finish or is it very shiny or glossy? Is the untouched surface allowed to remain the way it came from the mold, encrusted in some intrinsic way, such as cracked, mottled, wrinkled, corrugated?

Is the surface smooth or is it carved? Do light and shadow add to the quality of the candle's surface by creating highlights with light bouncing off the surface or outlines as shadows trapped in crevices?

Are elements of the surface design repeated around the candle or is the surface design a single, unique form? Is the surface design formally organized into patterns such as stripes, rows of shapes repeating, concentric rings or is the surface design a random distribution of texture, color, or pattern?

Lacy, tall, and delicate, this candle requires a base that is broad, sturdy, and simple. The busy pattern of the candle would not look good with a base that would also beckon for attention.

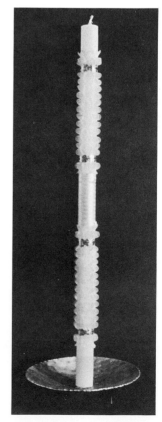

Folk art from Barcelona, Spain, finds its way into candle form. The decorations are hand painted.

A pitchfork inspired this candle of Scandinavian origin.

This candle was derived from a pinecone concept.

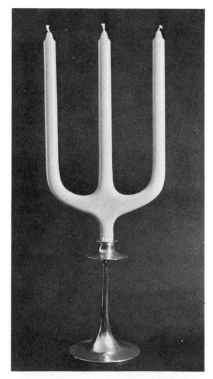

Color

Color evokes mood and can symbolize an occasion. Some colors are subtle and soft, others are startling, contrasting, and exciting. White signifies marriage, whereas blue denotes peace. A light yellow green means spring and bright red evokes strong emotion and a feeling for drama. Colors also can be decorative by blending or contrasting with the room environment.

Is your color transparent or densely opaque? Is it pastel, dull, and subdued or intense, bright, and screaming? Do your colors blend in chromatic-analogous variations such as yellow, orange, red; blue, blue green, green; red, red violet, blue; etc., or do they oppose one another by being complimentary such as red and green, yellow and violet, blue and orange? Do your colors blend or fuse together or are they clearly demarcated so that you can see the separation between colors? What happens to your colors in a brightly lighted room or at night when the candle is lighted?

Organization of Elements

All the above elements can vary by the way parts are combined. Arranging and rearranging shapes, colors, textures, and patterns lead to new design ideas. Grouping of candles by varying sizes and colors can also create other effects. Organization of parts brings order to these multiple design considerations.

Look at your candle as one object and notice how it relates to the shapes around it. See whether you can combine elements into predominantly horizontal, vertical, or diagonal groupings. Change and vary the height or position of your elements. If it is a group of candles, try standing one or two on boxes or blocks that will raise the candle to different heights. Try grouping by similarity with all the same color, or size, or shape. Try to create a rhythm of repeated elements or candle forms. Variations in color, shape, size, spacing, and directions will help you achieve rhythm and yet keep unity in your organization of forms or in the elements within a single form. Another system of organization can aim for contrast by contrasting size, darkness and lightness, forms, textures, directions. Try here to have a center of interest or focus or have one aspect dominate.

Overall designs work well on these three candles. The one in the foreground is hand carved. The other two are molded and then hand decorated with two paint treatments, antiquing (left) and coating (center).

Positioning of color and repeating of forms tied together physically and visually by a network of brown wax becomes an innovative candle form by Eric and Barbara Zelman.

Lee Weber's candle shapes have beautiful contours. If they had decorations applied to the surface, the purity of their forms and proportions would be lost. *Courtesy Lee Weber*

Beeswax molded into textured strips and adhered in overlapping diagonals provides an allover textural pattern in an analogous progression of colors in repeating sequences.

Specks of powdered color moved into patterns as this candle was dipped.

This hand decorated round block candle has a wax design in **Joseph's** coat colors that will keep its integrity as a design form even when the candle is two inches high.

Simple texturing of softened wax into a subdued corrugated effect becomes a very effective and distinctive surface treatment.

At any stage of burning this hand-carved candle will be attractive. The concentric rings are arranged so that the candle takes on a new design aspect as the candle burns.

Various implements such as a saw blade (candle on the left) and a baby's comb (candle on the right) can create beautiful surface variations.

Housekeeping and the Candle

Wick Maintenance

Charring the wick makes it easier to light; therefore, do not break off the charred end of the wick.

A candlewick that is too long will burn with much soot; cut the wick back from time to time. Keep the wick trimmed to ½ inch, but allow it to cool before trimming and re-lighting.

When extinguishing the candle flame, dip the wick into the melted wax and straighten it right away. This prevents sooting or smoking.

The Candle

Clean soiled candles by rubbing them with an old nylon stocking or with very little salad oil on a very soft cloth.

Remove match particles or wick debris from the top of the candle, particularly around the wick, because these particles may ignite and burn another depression in the candle.

Seal tapers in a waterproof polyethylene bag and store them in the refrigerator or deep freeze hours before use. They will burn more slowly and evenly.

If the candle flame flickers, and it is not because of the wick, trim excess wax off the sidewall *above* the burning level while the candle is warm from burning. Allow the wax pool around the wick to harden and then trim the wall more finely with a sharp knife.

Candles must stand upright, except for very slim tapers.

Dripless candles will stay dripless only if they are kept free from drafts or air currents, crooked wicks, excessive heat, such as grouping too many candles together, tilting.

Colors in candles are not fade-proof. Candles will fade if left out for extended periods of time. They are meant to be used and enjoyed; not to last forever.

Fragrances in candles also diminish when exposed to air for a long time, but lighting the candle will release the fragrance.

Store candles flat and in a cool, dark place to prevent warping and fading.

Candleholders

To remove wax from candleholders, rinse under very, very hot water.

Wax can be removed from glass holders or votive glasses by wiping with tissue saturated with cleaning fluid or rubber cement thinner (carbon tetrachloride). Keep these volatile solvents away from flames. (Remove wax from tablecloths or clothing by sandwiching the cloth between paper towels and pressing with a hot iron. Or a dry cleaner can easily remove wax.)

A bit of water in the bottom of the votive glass will prevent the wax from sticking and the glass from cracking (because of an over-heated metal disc that holds the wick).

Beware of flammable candleholders, made of wood or those made of certain flammable plastics, if the candle is the type that burns to the end and its flame will have a chance to touch the holder.

If your candle does not fit the candleholder because the candle base is too large, trim it with a sharp knife under hot water. If the candle base is too thin, wrap aluminum foil or a polyethylene strip around the base, or press a coil of putty or clay around the candle to fit the extra space.

Candle Use

Candles sitting no higher than lip level emit the softest most flattering glow at a dinner table.

A candle flame can absorb smoke and household odors and help to freshen a stuffy or crowded room.

Lighted candles add a warm glow to any room setting.

Attractive candles can attract attention and detract from less desirable features in a room. An underlighted room can have an undesirable effect on some people, particularly if they want to read or look closely at something.

Surface treatments — hand carving,
whipped wax and engraving.

All of these candles were made from
RTV silicone molds of crystal containers;
most of them by George and Irene Kinzie.

Painted candles from Spain in folk art line up.

Various decorating techniques—dripping
wax, brushing and scraping, designs with
sheets of wax, découpage, and applied
hand-molded shapes.

Contemporary arrangement.
Three candles from Spain.

A high keyed, very sophisticated arrangement
featuring Betty Thomforde's ice candle.

Different textural qualities — rolled beeswax,
handcrafted carved form, and cast gold foil.

Driftwood candle by Thelma R. Newman.

Like a fire in a fireplace, a lighted candle seems to say welcome, and watching a candle flame at the end of a tense day can help a person to relax and unwind.

Using candles properly in your environment finally depends upon your good taste, good sense, and some restraints. Everything has its limits.

The candle is the medium that holds this message. "Peace" is designed with typographical variations as an overall pattern, white on white.

Candle wax naturally drips. Here the texture of wax was deliberately built into the surface.

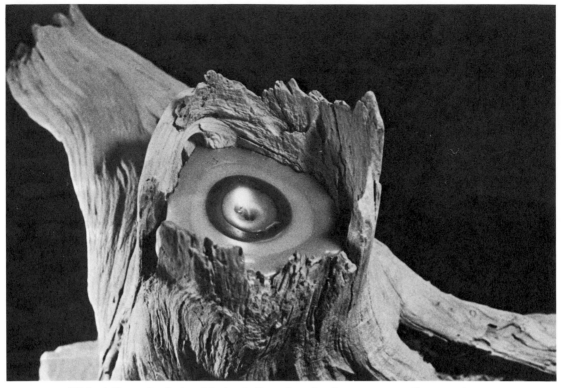

This driftwood piece with its hollow interior became a candle container. The pattern of the candle at the top was formed by varying the greens each time the wax was poured to fill the voids that develop around the wick. The form is large—3′ wide x 18″ deep x 24″ high. The size of the wick will predetermine that the candle flame will not touch the driftwood. As the candle burns a shell of wax will remain.

4

Finishing and Ornamenting

ONE NEED NOT USE WAX in order to ornament a candle. In fact, because some household materials are utilized, ornamenting the candle surface may be a good beginning point for someone starting to work with candles. Creative exploration here has great potential. Results can be very personal and expressive. Colors and designs can be varied endlessly. The following techniques of ornamentation are meant only as springboards to propel you onward to new variations in designing with candles. Many deal with essential concepts in crafts that are translatable to candlemaking. Some you may have used already and will feel competent to translate to candlemaking.

The first section here deals with "waxless" decorations. Waxless, though, in some cases, is a relative statement because some wax ma-

terials are used, but they are not traditionally wax candlemaking supplies. Most of these methods employ substances that are used for some other purpose. Magazine photographs become decoupage shapes; a doily and spray paint are used to stencil a design; melted crayon scraps become candle paint. A knife or linoleum cutting tool becomes a valuable wax carving implement, and so on.

Another section of "waxless" decorations utilizes hot and tepid water as a vehicle to create designs. Sometimes professional equipment is shown, but adaptations are very easy to accomplish. My candle dipping tube, for instance, was professionally made, but a tall can garnered from a restaurant could serve that purpose. Soldering two cans together with a high heat solder would give you a taller form for longer candles. Variations in the use of equipment and tools are illustrated here.

When utilizing overall designs it is advisable to use your rejected candles for this purpose. Candles that have surface blemishes can become beautiful forms if decorated.

The second section progresses with increasingly difficult techniques to the use of melted wax, wax sheets, and/or requires that heat be applied in some way on the candle.

Select, assemble, and carefully cut out magazine pictures.

"Waxless" Decorations Using Other Purpose Materials

THE DECOUPAGE EFFECT

Materials

> basic plain candle that is wide enough
>   to leave a shell when burning
> magazine pictures
> Mod-Podge or polyvinyl
>   acetate/chloride
> brush
> scissors
> yarn (optional)
> rubber cement (optional)
> sandpaper (optional)

About the Process

Decoupage is the technique of decorating with the use of paper cutouts. Magazine photographs work well because they have enough body not to wrinkle and are thin enough not to create too much bulk.

Sanding the edges of the underside of the cut pieces is optional. It helps to make edges blend into a unified whole.

Practice fitting your assemblage together. Trim and adjust until you are satisfied that the candle will not gape through because you cut a piece too short.

Spray rubber cement (optional) or paint Mod-Podge or p.v.a. over your candle surface.

Starting at one end, carefully place your largest background piece on the candle and as you attach this piece rub out air bubbles with your fingers.

Coat this background piece with Mod-Podge, etc. Although this water soluble material brushes on in milky streaks, it soon dries to a clear surface. Many layers of Mod-Podge can be built up, each drying to a clear gloss.

Apply your next cutout carefully rubbing out all bubbles.

Again, coat the next piece and so on until all cutouts have been added. Then paint the entire surface once or twice more, each time waiting for the previous layer to dry to a tacky finish.

Yarn coated with Mod-Podge was added to accent the design. This is optional. Fabric, metallic trim, and other flexible materials can be added the same way. When finished with this assemblage of materials, coat the entire form again. Overnight it will dry to a hard, ceramic glazelike surface.

The completed decoupage candle. Decoupage becomes an attractive container that encompasses a candle.

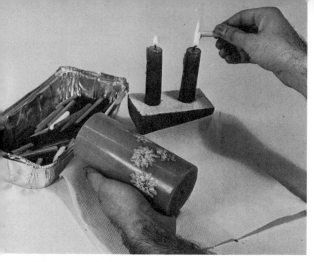

Plan your design. Select a background color. Dip the tip of your crayon into the candle flame.

Immediately apply, with light pressure, the melted crayon wax to the candle surface. If you leave the crayon in the candle flame too long, the wax will become coated with soot and discolor. Use short strokes and short intervals for crayon melting. If soot forms, quickly rub off with a rolling turn on a paper towel before applying the rest of the melted color to the candle.

ENCAUSTIC PAINTING

Materials

plain basic candle
old candle and holder for use of
candle flame
waxy crayons—scrap or otherwise—
without paper covering

About the Process

Plan your design. Consider that crayons can produce colorful impasto effects. The thickness of your design will depend upon how many layers of built-up wax you use. Try to coordinate and harmonize colors with the background of your candle. Start with general background colors first and gradually overlap colors in short strokes until you reach highlights and details on the last layers.

The completed crayon encaustic design using a floral motif. Tactile qualities are very pleasing and light picks up the texture in a very different way than on the contrasting smooth candle surface.

An old engraving that shows how candles were hand painted in the eighteenth and nineteenth centuries.

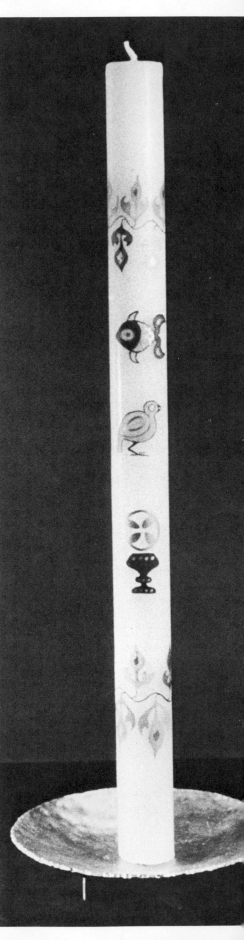

This church candle from Barcelona, Spain, was decorated with traditional oil paints thoroughly mixed with copal varnish via palette knife on a slab. Use a long hair sable brush. Copolymer paints using acrylic or acrylic-vinyl combinations are also good candle-painting vehicles. All candle paint can be scratched off because of the nature of the wax base form.

MELTED CRAYON

Materials

basic plain candle
crayon melter (or small aluminum muffin tin resting on an aluminum cookie sheet that sits directly over a heat source)
waxy crayon scraps
cotton swabs or brush

About the Process

Melted pools of color can be applied by brush or cotton swabs. I prefer cotton swabs because they are disposable. Use a different swab for each color. If you want very fine detail, however, a brush will be preferable. You can clean your brush in carbon tetrachloride or alcohol.

Plan your design. If you use cotton swabs, the pattern will not be exact. Arrange your colors in individual melting containers. Errors can be corrected by scratching away your crayon color from the candle surface and reapplying the corrected color.

Assemble materials and plan your design. Place crayon scraps into the crayon melter, or melt them in individual tins that are protected from direct heat (flammability) by an aluminum cookie sheet. Allow the crayons to melt into pools of wax color.

Apply your design with a cotton swab that has been dipped into the molten color. Corrections can be made by scratching away mistakes.

This candle wears the colored stripes of Joseph's coat. The overall texture and pattern is very pleasing to touch and to see.

Cut masking tape into the desired shape and place in a pleasing relationship on your candle. Make certain that the edges stick down securely.

RUB'NBUFF WAXY COATING

Materials

basic plain candle
masking tape
scissors
knife
Rub'nBuff

About the Process

Masking tape is used to block off areas of color. Plan a simple shape that is easily cut and attach it in an overall design. Rub'nBuff is very easily applied, best by fingertip. Since Rub'nBuff and similar products are of a wax base, they adhere with no trouble to the compatible wax surface of the candle.

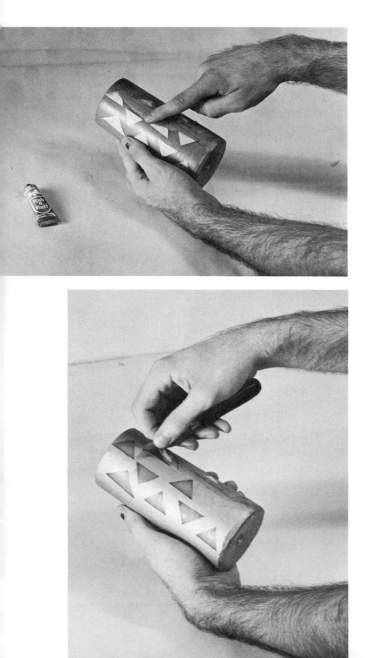

Via fingertip, apply a coating of Rub'nBuff. If edges of the masking tape lift up, apply the waxy coating outward from the tape rather than rubbing color toward the edges of the tape.

After a few minutes of drying, carefully lift the tape away.

The completed candle has a metallic blue matte coating with a glossy green wax finish in the triangular shapes.

Gold Rub'nBuff was applied in broad strokes with a soft cloth. Then excess was buffed away leaving this textured finish. Red glossy apples were pinned to the candle in sections with small straight pins so that the pinheads would not show. As the candle burns down, a section of apples will be pulled away one at a time.

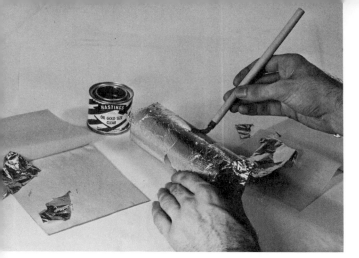

Apply gold size (spirit varnish) to your candle in the appropriate design. Allow it to dry until it is tacky. Then lift the gold leaf away from its package with a knife or brush and apply it to the candle surface.

As shown here, the leaf is very fragile. Don't sneeze or your design will blow away.

GOLD/SILVER LEAFING

Materials

Traditional Approach

> *basic plain candle*
> *gold size*
> *gold/silver leaf—real or imitation*
> *sable brush*
> *mastic varnish*

Contemporary Approach

> *Elmer's Glue or Mod-Podge*
> *brush*
> *gold/silver leaf*

About the Process

Gold leaf is a very old technique that has been used for centuries to decorate candles. It looks and works best when applied in designs rather than in the overall application as seen in the first example; in the former, gold has a chance to complement the wax and to prove its function as a wax candle rather than as a gold or silver candle.

The gold and silver leaf is very fragile and thin and difficult to handle. Nevertheless, every scrap can be used by overlapping pieces.

Smooth down the leaf with a soft brush or puff of cotton. If you need to overlap pieces, then apply more size, allow it to become tacky, and apply the gold or silver leaf.

When finished, coat the entire candle with mastic varnish. I allowed the gold leaf to wrinkle (it wanted to do that anyway) into patterns. This candle combines both gold and silver leaf in an overlapping random pattern. If wax was allowed to show through, it would be a much more successful surface treatment.

For use of Easy Leaf (see Sources of Supply), a gold/silver leaf that has an easy-to-remove backing, paint the area that you want in gold with Mod-Podge or Elmer's Glue.

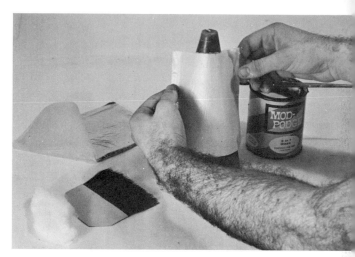

Immediately place the gold face of the Easy Leaf directly on the glue.

Gently press in place with a brush.

. . . or a puff of cotton.

Peel away the backing.

After the glue dries, brush away excess gold. Spots may be patched by adding more glue and Easy Leaf.

A flame crowns this festive form that is ready to grace a holiday arrangement.

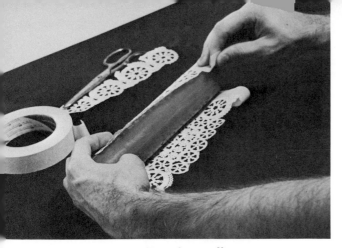

Fit your doily stencil to the candle.

Attach the doily with fine straight pins so that the doily lies flat. Mark ends with masking tape if a border is desired.

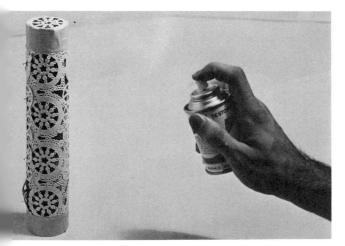

Spray with a continuous spray, moving the can top to bottom. Too much paint will cause paint to run under the stencil. It is best to apply light coats. Allow each coat to dry before applying the next until the desired depth of color is reached. Revolve the candle to complete the job.

STENCIL AND SPRAY

Materials

> basic plain candle
> doily or other flexible stencil form
> straight pins
> masking tape
> scissors
> compatible spray paint, lacquer type such as *Testor's Spray Paint for models*

About the Process

This is a very simple and effective ornamentation if an intelligent selection of colors is made. Keep coloring simple and allow the wax to show through. Before spray painting, test your spray paint on the base of the candle for its ability to dry. If it remains tacky after the usual drying time indicated by the manufacturer, then try another brand.

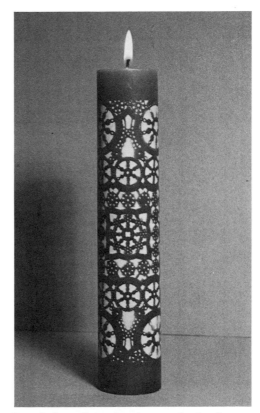

Just before the paint is completely dry remove the stencil and enjoy the "surprise" design. This white design on a red candle makes for a very attractive Christmas candle.

Light the sealing wax "candle" and anchor the sealing wax by dropping the very hot wax onto the appropriate spot on the candle.

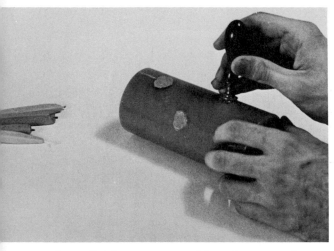

Immediately press your seal into the wax and allow it to remain there until the melted wax under the sealing wax has cooled and hardened.

SEALING WAX AND SEAL

Materials

> basic plain candle
> sealing wax "candles"
> sealing wax seal or other metal
>   implement

For Sealing Wax Flowers:

> mold form or spoon for flower form

About the Process

Sealing wax is another very old method of decorating candles. If you cannot get sticks of sealing wax (sold in card and gift shops), then try mixing your own from this old formula:

> 3 lbs. white beeswax
> 1 lb. pitch (rosin)
> coloring (powdered or oil)

Melt the ingredients and mold into a shape you can handle.

Pitch makes the beeswax soft enough to flow into a shape, sticky so that it attaches, and brittle when it has hardened.

A polka dot design was made with multicolored sealing wax. As the candle burns down, so will the decorations. The texture of the sealing wax is hard and glossy, against the satin smoothness of the candle.

Find a mold form such as an aluminum paint mixing tray or spoons and drip sealing wax into the center of the cavity. Then draw lines with the melting sealing wax out to the top of the cavity to create a petal pattern. Remove the flower after the wax has cooled.

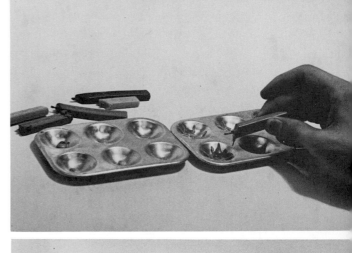

Anchor a small drop of hot sealing wax on the candle and immediately press the flower form into it. Allow slight pressure to remain until the candle wax under the piece has hardened. Leaves were dripped directly onto the candle.

The flowers project away from the candle in a pleasing repeat design. Thin cardboard shapes can be coated with sealing wax and attached to the candle in the same manner as the flower for different effects.

CANDLE CARVING

Materials

> *basic plain candles*
> *marking pen, e.g. Magic Marker*
> *carving tools such as linoleum or*
> *   wood cutters, knife or razor blade*

About the Process

Wax is a beautiful carving material. It responds easily to a knife or sharp instruments. Errors can sometimes be mended by remelting wax into the error. Carved designs can be simple or very complex with intricate modulations.

If you end up with a carving that you would like to keep and create as a molded form, make a mold of it. There are several ways to reproduce a wax original. See Chapter 5 for methods.

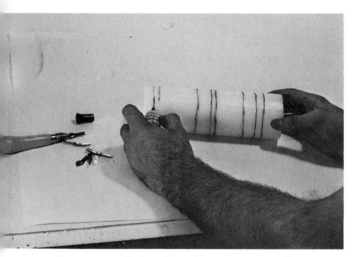

Draw your design directly on your candle with a Magic Marker or create your design on paper and then, with pinpricks, transfer the design to the candle by piercing the design lines at close intervals.

Carve your design with any knife tool. This form was carved with a linoleum cutter. The form is quite finished looking just as it is, or it can be dipped.

 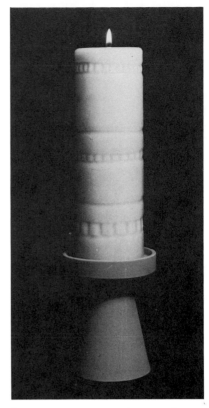

Carved candles may be dipped into a contrasting color of 200° F. wax—just once.

A greater amount of wax, hence color, collects in the carved areas, and sharp angles and edges are softened by the melting-coating process.

An assortment of carved candles. Only the candle with the bird design is an original. The others are made from molds. On the left, the candle, a buff color, was antiqued with a brown paint. Color was painted on and then rubbed off to highlight the raised areas.

Carved candles by Hallmark in a triangular shape that can be combined in many different mutlicandle effects.

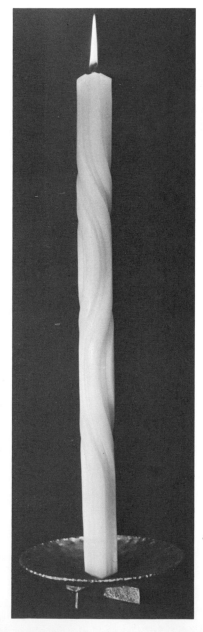

These candles from Israel were hand carved with simple line designs and then dipped into colors different from the base candle.

This is another version of a hand-carved candle from Spain.

TEXTURING WITH HEATED INSTRUMENTS

Materials

*saw or other potential texture-making
   metal form
hot plate or propane torch
basic plain candle*

About the Process

Look around for metal instruments that potentially can create texture effects in your kitchen or workshop. There are many. By combining texture effects, varying positions, and depths of pressure you can discover an amazing variety of surface treatments.

The hot plate is used to heat the saw. It is then pressed into the candle and drawn away. Before reheating the saw, wipe it clean on a paper towel so that the wax does not ignite.

Textures can be as varied as the instruments and design treatments that you use. This is the result of using the heated saw.

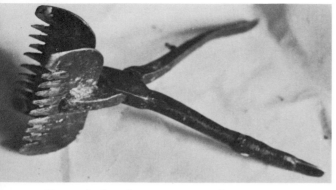

One of the instruments used to create pinched candle designs in southern Europe.

PINCHED DESIGNS

Materials

> basic plain candle
> forceps, tweezers, pliers
> water at 165°F.
> cold water

About the Process

Pinched candles are made throughout southern Europe. They are presently particularly popular in Spain and Mexico, and they have been developed into very elaborate and beautiful products.

After a bit of practice you will be able to make very attractive designs by varying the distance between pinches, angles, and spacing between lines, depth of the pinch and size of the instrument used.

Assemble all equipment. Dip candle section into hot water of 165° F. for just enough time to soften the surface.

Vary the size of your instrument as well as your angles and spacing. Repeat designs. If the wax gets hard, dip the candle into hot water again. Try to work quickly. It might be wise to practice this technique on an old candle first.

With warm pliers, forceps, or tweezers, immediately pinch the wax surface between your tweezers. The deeper you press the instrument into the wax, the deeper the petal.

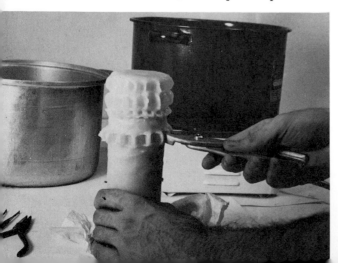

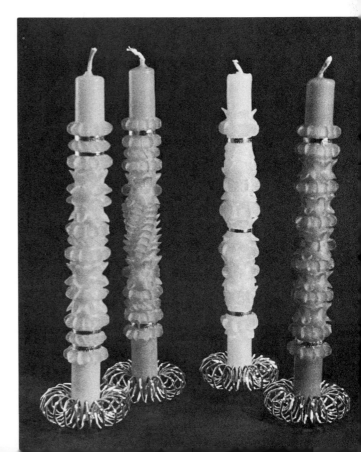

After all the pinching has been done, quickly dip the candle into hot water for a second if you wish to smooth out roughnesses. A final dip into cold water will keep petals fixed and nondrooping.

Cylinder candles in a pinched design from Barcelona, Spain. Gold paper was added to accent horizontal bands.

More delicate tapers in translucent pastel colors and in varying patterns begin to describe the wide variations possible with this technique.

MARBLING

Materials

> *cylinder or can of tepid water*
> *oil paint*
> *turpentine*
> *tongue depressors*
> *basic plain candle*

About the Process

Marbling is another old method of decorating, usually paper, but it can be applied to candlemaking. The technique described pictorially is an adaptation of this older method:

Soak gum of tragacanth until gelatinous.

Spread out the gum of tragacanth in a flat tray.

Thin oil paint with turpentine until the paint will drop off a tongue depressor.

Drop paint in varying amounts and colors on the gum of tragacanth.

With a stick move the oil paint into designs—try to repeat your patterns.

Holding your candle with ends between both hands, roll the candle on the surface of the gum of tragacanth in a continuous movement until the entire candle has been covered. Remove and allow the oil paint to dry.

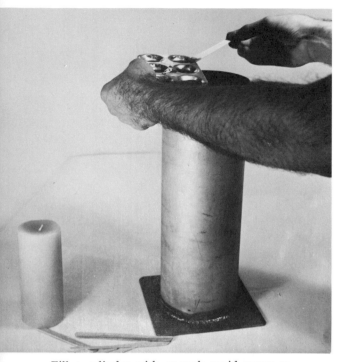

Fill a cylinder with enough tepid water to accommodate the length of your candle without water spilling over the sides. Your cylinder should also have enough surface to draw a complete marbling effect in one dipping. Prepare oil paints with enough turpentine so that the oil paint will drop off a tongue depressor.

Cover the entire surface of the water with random droplets of color. Be careful not to disturb the surface tension of the water since that is what keeps your color from sinking. With a stick you can manipulate the design or set it into a slight swirling motion.

Slowly dip your candle into the cylinder in one easy downward motion.

The colors and patterns of this marbling design are very subtle. You can achieve brighter and bolder effects by beginning with brighter colors.

And quickly lift the candle out.

Decorating with Wax

BRUSHED WAX TEXTURING

Materials

> *stiff brush such as a toothbrush*
> *baby comb—fine-toothed*
> *hot wax—clear and colored*
> *basic plain candle*

About the Process

This is just one of many ways to create an allover texture effect using hot wax, the natural texture produced by a stiff brush and color.

With a stiff brush apply 150° F. clear wax in short strokes to your colored candle until the entire candle has been colored. Then, using another color, overlap more brushstrokes. With a fine-toothed baby comb scrape away some wax in short random strokes creating a superimposed pattern on the brush marks.

This handsome texture is clear and green over a deep blue basic candle.

DRIPPING TEXTURE

Materials

hot wax in colors
a spouted can, regular can, or table-
spoon
waxed paper
basic plain candle

About the Process

Dripping is a natural texture for a candle—many candles with improper wick size or those that sit in a draft drip anyway. Variation is possible by using different colors, covering certain areas of the candle, or tilting the candle so that the wax drips down the side in a spiral effect.

The candle, which is resting on waxed paper to catch the drippings, is tilted so that the 165° F. wax will run down the sides of the candle in a spiral effect. By varying the amount poured, the length of the drips may be controlled.

Three colors, peach, orange, and fuchsia, were dripped over a white background.

Hot wax can be spooned over the top until it runs down the sides in straight lines. *Courtesy Gulf Oil Corp.*

Two other wax drip variations from Barcelona, Spain. The candle on the right was dipped after the dripping texture was created.

MASK-COATING

Materials

> *basic plain candle*
> *masking tape*
> *long pan—2" longer than candle and*
>   *2" deep*
> *hot wax*
> *2 corn holders or nails*

About the Process

All types of hard-edge designs can be taped onto a basic candle, and then the candle can be dip coated in a cylinder of hot wax (200°F.) or this alternate method can be used as described here. Certainly, no elaborate equipment is necessary to coat a candle with hot wax.

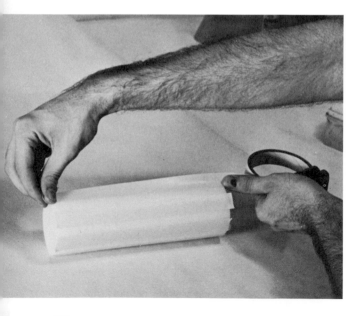

Cut and apply your masking tape to your candle in a design.

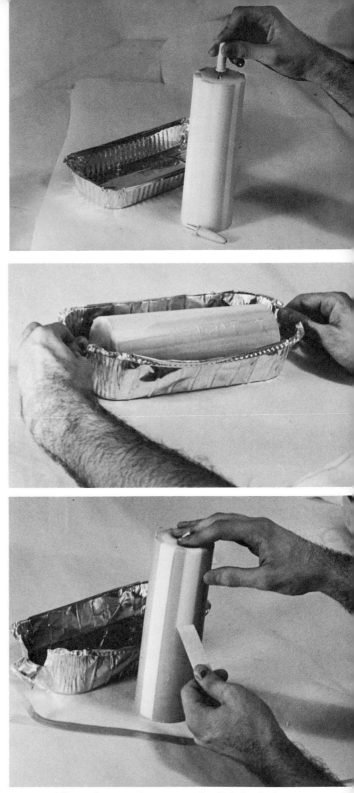

Attach corn holders or nails to the ends of the candle to act both as rollers and as handles with which to revolve the candle in the hot wax.

Cut a notch in the aluminum pan to accommodate the holders or nails. Pour in hot wax 220° F. (a bit hotter than the cylinder since more surface area is exposed to the air) and evenly rotate the candle in the hot wax. As soon as one revolution is completed, remove the candle.

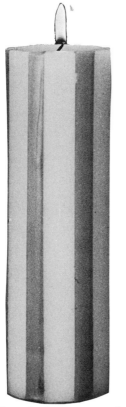

A very simple technique can produce a very effective design such as this orange and white striped candle.

Allow the coating to cool slightly before peeling away the masking tape, but do not wait for the coating to get cold because it will be too brittle to strip away the tape.

Dip or roll-coat your candle in a contrasting color. Plan and scratch your design into the surface coating, then scratch through the coating until the base candle color shows through.

ENGRAVING

Materials

> basic plain candle
> hot wax for dipping
> knife, linoleum cutter, nail
> nylon stocking

About the Process

Engraving is a very delicate technique that requires a different base candle color than its thin wax coating. Any pointed instrument can scratch through the coating. Errors can be patched somewhat with heat.

Polish to a lustrous sheen with a nylon stocking.

The engraved candle and its design inspiration—a fern.

DECORATIVE PATTERNS WITH MOLDING WAX

Materials

> *molding wax*
> *heat pen*
> *scissors, knife*
> *glass plate or cookie sheet*
> *nail with or without a head*

About the Process

To make hand-formed elements of wax use a soft-type wax such as beeswax sheet, as in these illustrations. A very good molding wax is:

> *4 parts beeswax to 1 part*
> *Turpentine (Turpentine of Venice)*

Stained-glass window makers of yester-year (and today, too) mixed beeswax with a small quantity of Venice Turpentine over heat until it dissolved and was thoroughly blended. When cool, small chunks of the mixture were kneaded in the hand until the material became ductile and sticky. The stained-glass window maker used this brownish wax as an adhesive to fix pieces of glass against his glass easel while working. The glass pieces remained fixed together until pried away.

For modeling, wax requires an elastic quality and some pressure or heat to adhere it to the candle base. Possibilities are enormous because you can roll, pinch, pull, twist, and combine the wax into units from basic shapes to free forms in any number of combinations.

For a sticky modeling wax, melt four parts beeswax to one part Venice Turpentine.

Mix the Venice Turpentine until it thoroughly dissolves. When cool, knead by hand into shapes. Color can be added before the mixture cools.

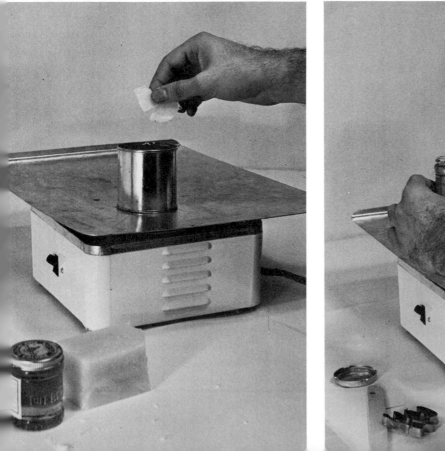

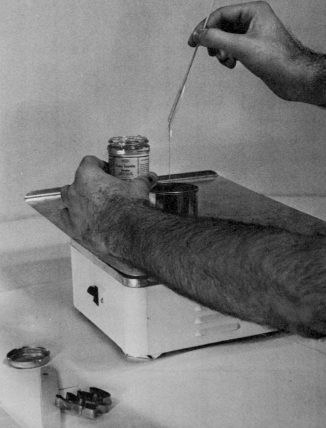

Cut your shape. Knead the wax in your hands until soft enough for rolling and shaping, or place in water no warmer than 104° F. When pliable, roll it with your hands on a smooth surface such as a piece of glass or cookie sheet until the substance becomes cordlike.

Press onto the candle and if it does not stick use a heat pen to affix the pieces.

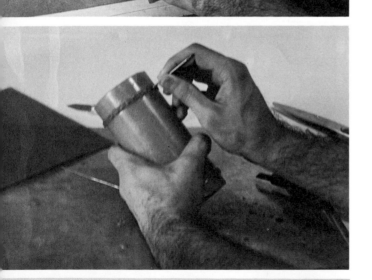

To add a decorative interest that also helps adhere the wax strip, press a nailhead into the wax at intervals.

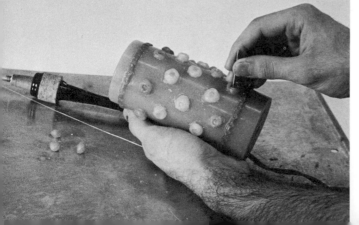

Try spacing concentric vertical strips around the candle. Or make circular, small wax balls and press shapes into the balls. Attach to the candle with a glutinous wax or heat pen. Try using other tools to make designs into the modeling wax, such as a knitting needle, palette knife, serrated knife, fork, and so on.

Floating shells and flower forms in a large punch bowl.

The pinched candle grows from the Spanish tin candle holder.

Layered free forms shaped with a propane torch closely resemble the petrified wood form on the right.

Pop candles shock one into laughter.

An assortment of very different techniques from a ball shell, a "cutglass" shape, a layered free form, a color burst to a corrugated layered candle.

Pinched candle designs from Spain and a yellow one described in detail within.

A candle with a gold wax rubbed surface, encircled with removable apples.

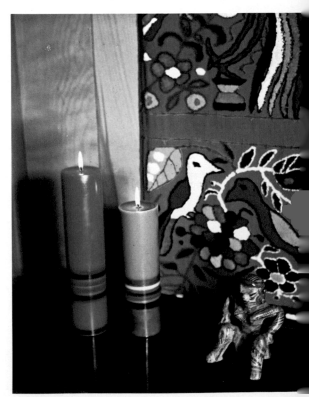

Environment for Floss Perisho's striped candles.

This is only one of many possible ways to decorate candles with modeling wax. Try free-form ornaments, dot clusters, spirals, pear shapes, cubes, cord effects, vertical stripes, and dots.

WHIPPED WAX

Materials

With Paraffin:

> *basic plain candle*
> *eggbeater*
> *tall 2 lb. coffee can*
> *cornstarch*
> *washing detergent (optional)*
> *hot paraffin*
> *tongue depressors, fork or other*
>   *applicator*

With Beeswax:

> *beeswax*
> *Turpentine of Venice*

About the Process

Whipped wax is a much abused technique used to make "sugarcoated" candles. It does cover a number of flaws and can be attractive if applied with restraint.

Whipping wax is as simple as beating an egg. Whip it quickly to a froth after the wax has cooled enough to form a surface skin. *Courtesy Gulf Oil Corp.*

Then immediately apply it with an implement such as a fork. *Courtesy Gulf Oil Corp.*

Whipped wax can be more professionally done. After your paraffin has melted, add one tablespoon of cornstarch per pound of wax so that the wax will stick to the sides of the candle better.

For added whiteness, add one tablespoon of washing detergent per pound of wax anytime during the whipping. Start whipping the wax as soon as a skim forms on its surface. The faster the beater is turned, the fluffier the wax.

When fluffy, daub the frothy wax with a fork, tongue depressor, or gloved finger onto the candle.

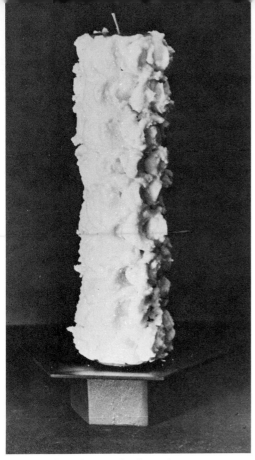

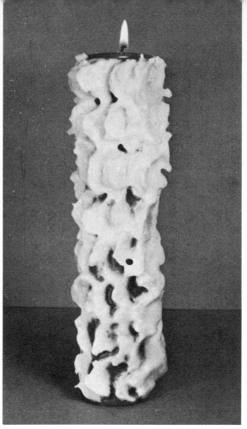

The surface is rough, but shows a repeat overlapping pattern.

A glazed surface can be effected by dipping the entire candle into a hot water (220° F.) bath or by dipping it into clear hot paraffin (200° F.).

A commercial operation where whipped wax is used.

Apply tape in a spiral design to your base candle. Color, and add one teaspoon of Venice Turpentine to 1 lb. of beeswax, and when a skim forms on the surface of the wax whip until fluffy.

Immediately apply the froth to your candle.

Roll your candle on a warm piece of plate glass so that the surface flattens.

88

Pull away the masking tape.

Although this decoration is made with bees-wax and Venice Turpentine, there is a commercial product called Whip-Wax, which is a wax liquid with adhesive properties that can be whipped, colored, and even applied with a cake decorator. (See Sources of Supply.)

This is a very decorative Christmas candle, inspired by the candy cane.

89

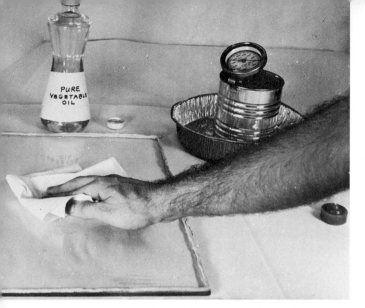

Pour your own sheet by edging a sheet of plate glass with Mortite (a prepared putty) to create a dam to hold the melted wax. Coat the glass with vegetable oil or spray with silicone.

DECORATIONS USING WAX SHEET

Materials

> basic plain candle
> plate glass sheet
> Mortite
> hot beeswax
> color
> flat metal strip
> metal-cutting tool
> heat pen
> knife
>   or prepared beeswax sheets

About the Process

Very beautiful and special candles can be made with the use of flat wax sheet ornamenting. A counterchange design concept was used here, contrasting yellow against orange, but shapes are endless and because of this, should be selected carefully. Repeating a shape is a safe way to end up with an attractive candle.

Pour colored beeswax at 150° F.

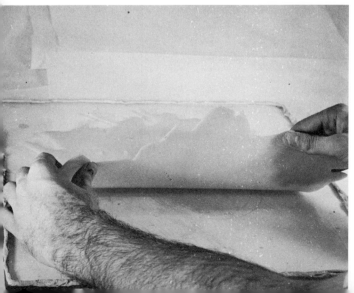

When the wax is pliable and yet solid enough to lift away from the glass it is ready for use. To shortcut the making of wax sheets you can use ready-made beeswax sheets.

With flat metal stripping form an outline of your design and tape the ends together so that it becomes a cookie cutter.

Press the cutter into the sheet and lift the cutout with a knife.

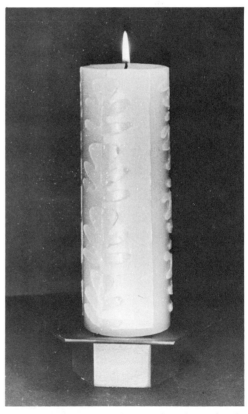

Attach the cutout to the candle with a heat pen or an adhesive type of wax.

The completed candle employed a simple concept called "counterchange" in a repeat design.

After releasing your basic candle from its mold, wipe away the silicone mold release material with alcohol.

DECORATING WITH CAST WAX ORNAMENTS

Materials

> *basic plain candle*
> *Mod-Podge, Elmer's Glue, or poly-
> vinyl chloride*
> *ceramic mold*
> *brush*
> *knife*
> *melted paraffin and color*
> *silicone spray*

About the Process

Many kinds of ornaments can be cast in commercial molds or in "found" molds and then applied to your candle, either as repetitive ornaments or as a single decoration.

Brush on Mod-Podge, Elmer's Glue, or polyvinyl chloride.

The basic candle, original mold, and Mod-Podge glazed candle. The glazed candle is complete in itself or the glaze can become an excellent base for affixing ornaments.

92

This ceramic mold leaves a beautiful finish on the wax. Spray lightly with silicone before pouring colored wax into its cavities.

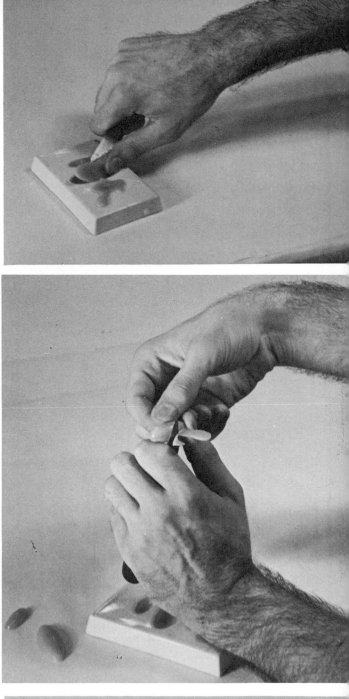

Release the ornaments from the mold and trim with a knife if necessary.

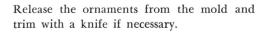

Coat the underside of the ornament with Mod-Podge, etc.

And attach it to your glazed candle.

Simple, but effective, wax gems adorn this colorful candle.

5

Making Molds for Candles

LEARNING HOW TO MAKE your own molds will liberate you from always using commercial mold forms and will permit more personal and creative development of forms. You can sculpture a beautiful shape, for instance, and want to preserve it by repeating it in production. Or you may find an object, used for some other purpose, such as a wood turning, that could become a handsome candle form and you may want to duplicate it. All this is possible with a variety of mold-making techniques—some more effective for certain shapes and still other methods more suitable and economical for different types of forms.

Some mold-making techniques are more difficult to execute than others. Two-part molds take more time than one-part molds. But two-part molds are easy to remove from the candle without surface injury to the wax, whereas in one-part molds it can be difficult to peel away the mold or to pry out the candle.

Costs of mold-making varies from very cheap clay and plaster to expensive plastic materials. All will be discussed here with strengths and limitations to help you make a decision as to which material and process to use.

COMMERCIAL METAL MOLDS

How to Use Them

When first using a metal mold, blow out any dust and then spray the mold with a

95

A commercial professional type mold from Italy. This is a two-part mold that screws together at the center with a nut and bolt. Wicking is inserted and held in place with a bar at the base of the candle, which is the mouth of the mold.

A spun aluminum mold that has no seams and produces a satin finish is manufactured for the McGowan's Candle Farm. They also distribute a taper-making machine called "the Little Dipper" that makes 15" tapers and holds 25 lbs. of wax.

coating of silicone. Do not use wax hotter than 175°F. in these molds. There is usually a hole at the base of the mold to accommodate the wick, and this is strung by stringing the wick through the hole and threading it through until it can be attached into a vertical, taut position at the top of the mold. Knot the wick at the bottom and seal the hole with sticky adhesive tape or Mortite. In releasing your candle never hit your mold so hard that dents will form. Wait for the wax to cool completely. Cooling normally takes from four to eight hours. If there is still sticking, then place your candle in the refrigerator for about five to fifteen minutes. Some people recommend cooling the mold at first by immersing it in a lukewarm water bath; they claim it produces a glossier candle. This is not necessary; if your mold has a glossy surface to begin with, your wax will duplicate it. If you use a water bath for cooling your candle only, keep the mold in the bath until wax hardens to about $\frac{1}{8}$" thickness.

To clean out wax that may have stuck to the mold use commercial solvents (or see solvent chart). Never scratch the interior of your mold with a sharp instrument. Not only will scratches show on the surface of your next candle, but the wax tends to stick to the scratches, making removal of subsequent candles more difficult. An alternate way to remove wax from your mold is to heat the exterior with a propane torch for a few seconds and allow the wax to drain out of the wick hole. If a torch is not available, bake the candle mold in a 200°F. oven for fifteen minutes. Make certain that a foil container is placed under the mold to catch melting wax.

COMMERCIAL PLASTIC MOLDS

How to Use Them

Commercial plastic molds are of many different kinds of plastics. They may be made of flexible vinyls, silicones or rigid polystyrenes, acetates, polyethylene, and polypropylene. These are the most popular types. They may be sleeve molds of one piece, open molds for shallow pourings, or two-piece molds for intricate carvings and candles with undercuts.

Some of these molds are originally made for plaster or polyester resin, but if they can withstand a temperature of 220°F. without deforming, then it is safe to use them with wax.

Flexible Molds

The making and using of flexible molds is described in detailed step-by-step photographs, except for *shallow* flexible molds. In that case employ the usual technique of spraying or coating your mold before pouring your wax. When the wax is completely hard and ready for removal, however, flex and then lift the mold *from* the wax and not the other way around. Otherwise your wax may deform or crack. To lift the mold away start at one corner and work your way around and then to the middle. Hold the rest of the mold down with the palm of your hand.

Rigid Plastic Molds

Many candle molds come in two pieces. Spray or coat the interior before joining the two halves. Use pressure clamps or rubber bands to hold halves together. To be certain your mold is seam tight, pour a higher melting-point wax into the mold first; if it does not leak, fine. Allow the harder wax to remain in the mold until it forms a $\frac{1}{16}$" to $\frac{1}{8}$" coating; pour out the rest. If there is seam leakage, pour the wax back into your pitcher immediately, and allow the wax that clings to the mold to harden. Then pour wax that is at least 25° cooler into the mold. Pour additional wax in stages so that the higher melting-point wax that is sealing the seams does not melt.

Another technique to prevent wax seepage is to tape the outside seams of your mold with sticky adhesive tape and then apply pressure clamps or rubber bands. If there is seepage, the flash of wax that is caused by the wax in the seams can be carved away when the candle hardens.

Do not be too hasty in removing your candle from your mold. Wait twelve to twenty-four hours if you want a stable candle.

Find a suitable container to support your glass mold, such as an egg carton. Warm the outside of your glass mold with hot water. Color your wax and pour it at 200° F. slowly into the mold trying to aim for the center. When partially solidified, pierce the center with an ice pick and refill with wax.

COMMERCIAL GLASS MOLDS

Commercial glass molds are meant for casting either polyester resin or wax. Most are waste molds because they have to be broken to remove the form. They are usually made of a very thin type of glass. Typical of these are the glass ball and blown glass shaped molds shown here.

About the Process

Glass imparts a beautiful sheen onto wax. If a glass form is particularly desirable and you want to use it continuously, it may be wise to make a two-part RTV (room temperature vulcanizing) silicone mold of it. (See instructions further on in this chapter.) Take particular care when breaking away the glass not to shatter it into fine slivers that could become embedded in the wax.

Consider these small wax castings not only as single units but as aggregates that can be built upon and clustered.

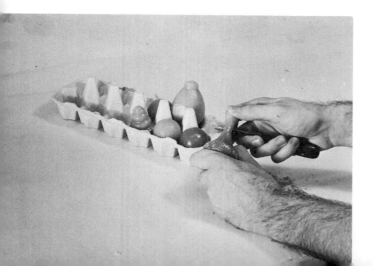

To remove from the glass, submerge the entire form—glass, mold, and wax—in cool water as soon as the wax has solidified. Keep it there for about five minutes. This will cause the wax to contract. Then place the mold in a plastic bag and tap it with a hammer until the glass falls away. If you use too much pressure, spicules of glass will cling to the wax. Trim the neck away.

 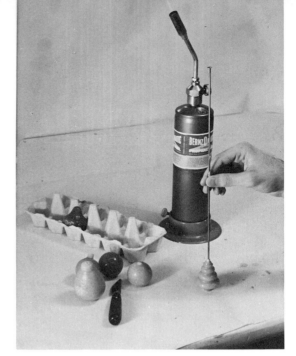

Rotate the needle slightly and withdraw it. Then tie a knot into a wick, dip it in wax for stiffening, and string it through the wick hole.

With a hot knitting needle or ice pick pierce a hole through the form.

Various Lilliputian forms in a holiday arrangement.

Aggregates of small forms create multiple wick arrangements. They can be clustered or built upon.

A Finnish candle design that requires the neck to remain on the ball. This projection fits into the candleholder. With it are some glossy small ball candles from Spain.

FOUND MOLD FORMS— IMPROVISED MOLDS

Any container that does not have undercuts can potentially become a mold if it will not melt away with a pouring of wax at a minimum of 130°F. The potential range is tremendous. Paper, cardboard, plaster, metal, plastic, ceramic, wood—anything can become a candle mold as long as you can remove the wax when it becomes hard.

You can use paper cups, milk cartons (support these with a crisscross of string or masking tape), cardboard tubes (seal one end), cardboard boxes, tin cans, funnels, plastic containers such as bleach bottles, antiques, wood molds, jello molds, eggshells, and so on.

How to Use Paper Product Molds

Make certain that corners and edges are reinforced with tape. Then support large spans by tying cord or taping masking tape around the sides for support. A vegetable oil coating applied on all inside nonwaxed surfaces comes next (milk cartons do not need this). Do not pour wax hotter than 190°F. into paper and cardboard, and for milk cartons keep the temperature at about 165°F. even though your surface will be dull. To keep bubbles from collecting on the surface, stir the wax in its mold with a tongue depressor. Then allow the wax to solidify undisturbed, but fill the cavity depressions as needed. Wick holes can be punctured later.

The jello mold had semisphere depressions that were first filled with wax after the mold was spray-coated with silicone.

Wax at 190° F. was poured into the mold after the first decorative pouring (of another color) had hardened.

When the wax hardened it was removed, and wick holes were pierced in the wax with a hot knitting needle. A wire wick was then strung into each hole.

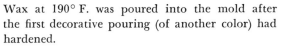

This multiple-wick candle serves as a festive centerpiece.

How to Use Metal Molds Such as Jello Molds

Metal jello molds, in fact any metal or plastic form from tin can to plastic bottle, can be treated in the following way. There is nothing special about the process.

EGGSHELLS AS MOLDS

How to Use Them

Tap the large end of your egg gently to crack a bit of the shell, enough to make a hole of about ¾″ across. This end of the egg has an air pocket. Then shake the egg from the shell and rinse the inside with cold water.

Stand the egg upright, hole to the top, in an egg carton, and fill it with melted wax.

An egg takes anywhere from ¼ to ⅓ cup of wax. Pierce a hole when the wax has hardened partially and fill in depressions with the wax. When the wax has cooled and cured, peel away the shell. Pierce a hole with a hot knitting needle, thread your wick, and make a base by cutting a small circle of felt or cork and gluing it with Elmer's Glue or rubber cement to the bottom of the egg shape.

For a variation try filling the egg with one color, perhaps white or brown; let that harden to a ⅛″ shell and pour out the rest of the wax. Then fill the shell with white wax and let that harden until almost completely hard. Scoop out a ball from the center and fill with yellow wax. When that has hardened, fill it again with white wax. After all this hardening you will have a hard-boiled egg.

MUD AND SAND AS MOLDS

Sand Molds—About the Process

Sand candles that utilize a cavity in sand as a mold are described fully in Chapter 6. If sand is fully saturated with water and wax is poured at 165°F., very little sand will remain on the candle. Whatever does stick can be brushed and washed off. Shapes with undercuts in any design that can be scooped out of the sand are feasible for one-time molds.

Carve a negative shape into moist ceramic clay.

Insert your wick and pour wax at about 165° F.

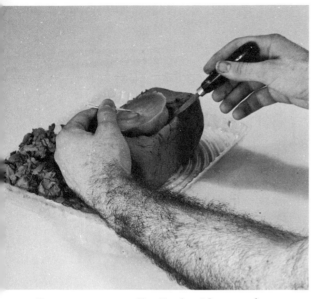

Remove your candle. It should come from the mold with very little clay sticking to it. The rest can be washed away.

This is a small amorphic shape, waxlike and molten-looking with a very efficient flame.

All you do to remove the candle is clear away the sand and pull out your candle. If you do not like the sandy or dull texture after cleaning and washing away the wax, dry the candle and dip it into wax at 220°F.

Mud Molds—About the Process

Mud modes are my favorite mold material. "Mud" actually is unfired ceramic clay that is soft enough to carve. It is particularly good because every detail reproduces into the wax and because the clay can be carved into any shape. Undercuts are possible. The clay has complete flexibility. Besides carving forms into a clay block, coil or slab forms can be built up into potential molds as long as there is enough support for the walls of the mold. Here again clay can be used to buttress the mold walls for strength.

If wax is poured at 165°F.–175°F., little clay sticks to the wax. The rest washes away. The candle polishes well

or can be dipped into a color bath of hot wax.

SMALL ORNAMENTS CARVED FROM PLASTER

About the Process

Small decorations that require repetitive casting can be carved from plaster. Pour plaster into a flat container that is deep enough to accommodate the depth of carving you desire. After the plaster has set up, carve your design into the plaster making certain that there are no undercuts.

Coat the mold with shellac that has been diluted ⅓ with alcohol. After the shellac dries, oil the mold or saturate it with water. Pour a flexible wax into the carved areas. (Your wax should be able to flex when warm without cracking.) When the wax forms are still warm, lift them out of the mold. Apply as soon as possible to your candle.

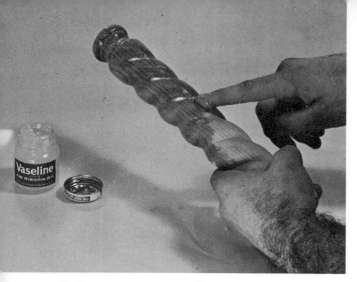

Find an appropriate candle shape, or carve your own. Coat it with Vaseline (petroleum jelly).

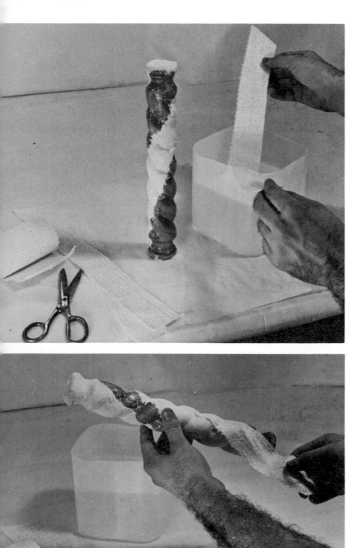

PLASTER BANDAGE MOLDS

About the Process

Pariscraft or plaster bandage that is used by doctors for wrapping broken limbs is a fine material for a mold—temporary or permanent if cast in plaster. Use a simple but appropriate form of any material. The entire process takes minutes compared with more involved mold forms.

Cut Pariscraft or plaster bandage into strips of 8"–10" and dip into water.

Wrap the saturated strips around your candle form.

104

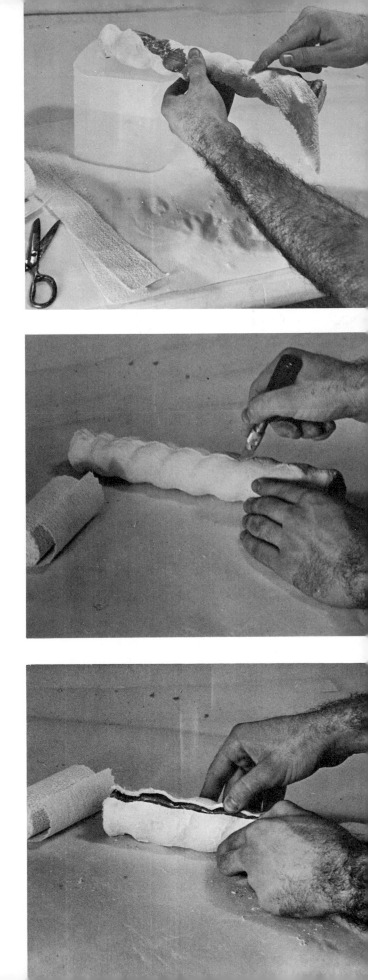

Work out any air bubbles. Take painstaking care to have the plaster strips conform exactly to the form. Apply two to three layers.

Allow it to set for ten minutes, and then cut the plaster form in half.

The plaster will still be soft after removing it from the mold form so take care to avoid distortion. Allow the sections to dry a bit before using the mold.

Coat the interiors with vegetable oil or spray with silicone. Assemble both halves, joining them with a sticky adhesive tape and/or rubber bands.

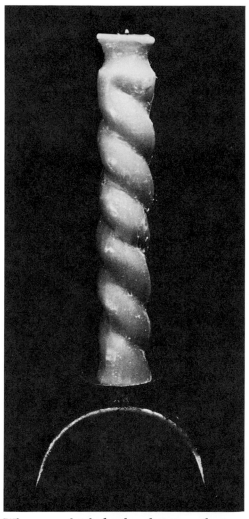

Support your mold and pour a high melting point wax at 185° F. If there are leaks, remove the wax and permit whatever wax remains to seal the seams. After it has hardened use a lower melting point wax at 145° F. to fill the mold.

When completely hardened remove the tape and rubber bands. This is the way the candle looked before seams were trimmed and before the candle was dipped into a hot wax bath.

CASTING IN PLASTER MOLDS

As described by Lee Weber of Montezuma, New Mexico.
All photographs in this series courtesy Lee Weber.

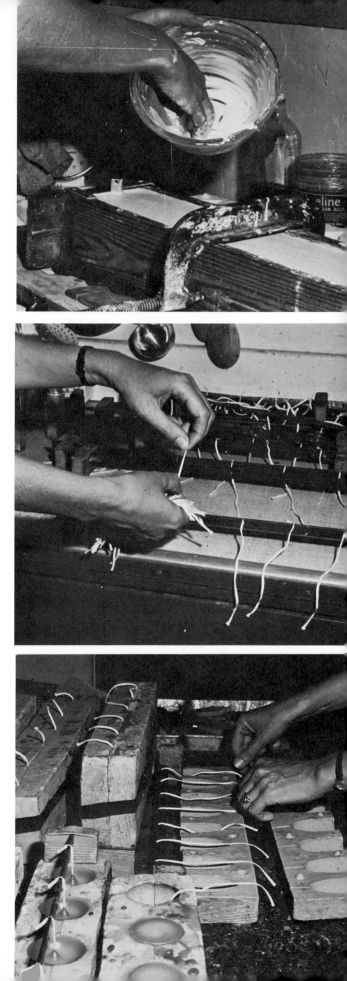

The molds are made of plaster and set up as gang molds in two halves. There are three, six, or eight cavities, depending on the size of the candle.

The wick is placed in slots in a metal frame, which is held in place above the center of each candle.

The wicking attached to the metal strip is placed between two halves of the mold.

The two halves of the mold are held in place with stout rubber bands (inner tube).

The bottom of the two-piece mold is sealed with wax to prevent run-through in the pouring.

The wax is then poured into the cavities and, when the wax has set sufficiently, the wicks are clipped from the bottom of the candles—freeing the metal frame. The shrink cavity is then filled.

108

When the candles are cold they are removed from the mold.

The cast mark is then trimmed from each candle.

The bottom of each candle is flattened on a heated metal surface.

109

The candles are then dipped into melted wax to give a smooth exterior finish.

The final step is snipping the wick to the proper length for burning.

A grouping of Lee Weber's very beautiful candle shapes. *Courtesy Lee Weber*

MAKING FLEXIBLE PLASTIC BLANKET MOLDS

About the Process

Flexible plastic molds are durable and can withstand very high pouring temperatures (400°F.). Several hundred castings can be made with these one-piece molds. Making the mold is a very simple operation. If the original candle form is an uncomplicated one, you can remove the cold candle as you would take a sock off of a foot, but if the original is complicated and has many undercuts, a slit will have to be cut into the mold to ease removal of the candle. Then, for subsequent pourings, a sticky adhesive tape should be used to rejoin the slit. Each time the mold is used, coat it with 50 percent green soap-water mixture or spray it well with silicone.

The original wooden mold positive is coated very well with a paste wax such as Butcher's wax.

Stretchy Adrub RTV was used to make this blanket mold. (See Sources of Supply.) Two parts by weight of Adrub RTV are placed in a preweighed paper cup.

Then one part by weight of the Adrub hardener is added.

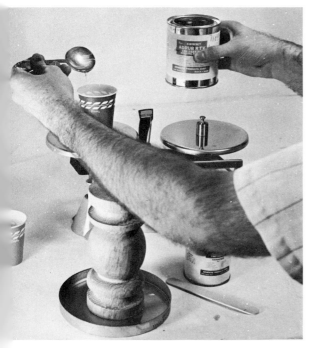

The mixture is stirred thoroughly for one to three minutes, taking care not to mix air into the mixture.

After mixing, brush the first coat over the mold. Turn it upside down to make certain no uncovered spaces remain.

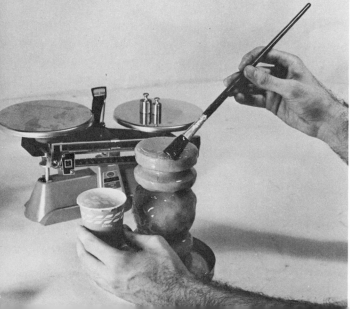

Subsequent layers (one or two more) can be brushed or poured over the form. Wait fifteen minutes between each layer. A flange is formed by some of the RTV "rubber" draining to the pan that holds the mold form. Do not make the mold too thick; it is not necessary and will impede removal. You may clean your brush with acetone. To remove the mold, if there are no undercuts, you can peel off the mold from the prototype by rolling it back as you would take off a sock. If this proves too difficult, then cut a slit down one side and remove the positive. To use, join the slit side with very sticky adhesive tape, such as duck tape, and make certain there are no leaks. You can test for leaks by filling the mold with water. (Be certain to dry the mold thoroughly before using mold release.)

In twelve hours the mold is ready to use. Support it in a can or box. Coat it with a green soap–water mixture or silicone.

At 200° F. pour your wax. A wick can be added beforehand by making a wick hole first and threading the wick the usual way.

When the wax is cold, peel off the mold as you would a sock. If you are afraid that pressure would break your candle, then cut a single slit part of the way down on one side and lift out the candle. For additional pourings, rejoin the slit side with adhesive tape.

This candle is burning with a Key-Wick (see Sources of Supply). It is a small circular carbon form with a center hole that is placed on top of the candle and lighted. As it burns, wax is melted and the wick sinks lower and lower into the candle. Key-Wick comes in various sizes. Supposedly reusable, they seem to last only for one candle.

Another mold made of Stretchy Adrub is supported for pouring.

The completed candles are small stalagmite-looking forms. Several hundred pieces can be made from this mold.

MAKING RTV SILICONE MOLDS

About the Process

The RTV silicones are excellent mold materials. They are easy pouring and flow to fill minute crevices reproducing exact details. Because of their ease of mixing at room temperatures, they have become very popular mold materials even though they are quite expensive. These silicone RTV's cure in unlimited thicknesses, remain resilient for hundreds of castings, and can accept heat up to 500°F. They are very exact and strong mold materials that come in various viscosities.

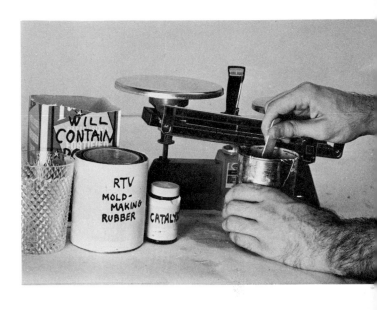

In order to make a mold of this crystal glass, only a one-piece mold is necessary. A container was found that would accommodate the glass without too much waste around the sides. Containers can be built with cardboard and masking tape. The silicone RTV will not stick to cardboard. One pound of RTV silicone produces twenty-five cubic inches of rubber. Silastic E, a medium viscosity RTV material from Dow Corning (see Sources of Supply), was used. One part, by weight, of catalyst was added to ten parts, by weight, of the base.

The two parts were mixed together thoroughly for at least two to three minutes with a clean tongue depressor. Care was taken not to entrap air in the mixture.

A base of Silastic was poured to ¼″ and allowed to cure for twenty-four hours. This provided a base for the glass to rest on. It was not worth preserving the plain bottom of the glass nor the clear band around the top, so the glass was placed in the mold right side up. Otherwise, the glass can be placed upside down in the container (no base of Silastic needs to be poured then), and the Silastic can be poured to ¼″–½″ over the top of the glass in one operation.

In order for additional layers of Silastic to adhere to cured Silastic RTV, a coating of RTV Silicone Primer, a pink liquid, was brushed on the rubber base.

The glass was placed into the container, exactly centered, right side up.

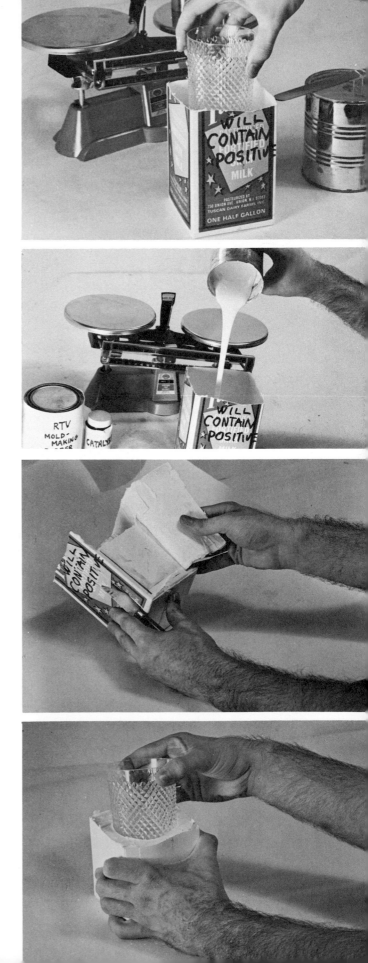

Additional Silastic E RTV was weighed, mixed, and poured. Pouring is critical. It is best to pour from at least 12″ to 18″ above the container. By stretching the mold material, many entrapped air bubbles are broken. Pour into one corner so that the material will flow upward; that way no air bubbles will be entrapped as the Silastic wraps itself around the positive.

The mixture remains workable for two hours and cures to a tack-free surface in twenty-four hours. Then the carton may be peeled away.

The crystal glass is removed.

Wax of 210° F. is then poured into the mold—which does not need to be precoated. Precoating, however, does preserve the mold for more production.

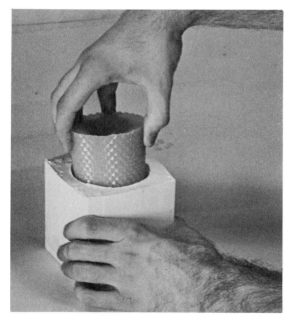

When cold, the candle is removed and a wick is added.

The completed candle is an exact reproduction, in wax, of the glass.

Candles made from RTV Silicone rubber molds by George and Irene Kinzie of Lyons, Colorado.

MAKING TWO-PART MOLDS

About the Process

For complicated shapes with undercuts or for molds made of rigid materials such as epoxies and plaster, two-part molds may be necessary. If the mold positive (male section) will become locked into the mold negative (female section), then either a very elastic mold material should be used, or a two-part mold should be made. Two-part candle molds are not difficult to make, but precision is necessary.

The method described can be used with plaster, epoxy, or RTV silicone molding rubber particularly. This is one of many approaches. With experience you will be able to vary this method.

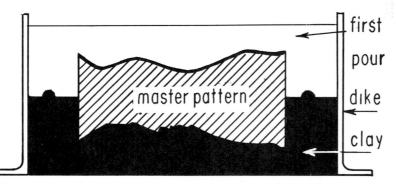

Find a container that is a little larger than your candle in all dimensions—at least ½" larger on all sides. This will become a dike to contain the mold material. Lay a bed of nonhardening type clay on the bottom of the box and press your mold (positive) into the clay halfway. Smooth out the parting line, which is the exposed area of the clay, with a knife or clay-working tools. And either add a coil or groove out a notch so that the two halves of the mold will match and lock together later. Coat your master pattern and clay bed (parting line) with release and make your first pouring of mold material until the mold material is ½" above the pattern. Allow the mold material to remain undisturbed on a level surface until it finally cures or hardens.

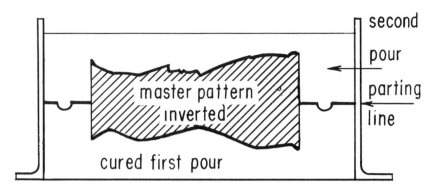

After the first pouring of mold material has hardened, turn the whole thing
—dike, pattern, and mold, upside down so that the first mold pouring is
now resting on the table. Remove the dike (without destroying it) and the
clay, but keep the pattern in place in the first half of the mold. Then reposi-
tion the box or dike so that the mold and pattern are reversed. The mold is
now in the bottom of the box and the pattern half is exposed on the top. Coat
the exposed part of the master pattern, the box, and the parting line with
release, and pour the second section of your mold material until it is about
1/2″ above your pattern.

When this part of the mold material has hardened, remove the master
pattern. Place the two halves together and secure with one or two rubber
bands. Drill a hole at one end to receive your wax. Remove debris caused
by the hole-making. Coat your mold with release. Clamp the two mold sections together with rubber bands and pour your wax. When the wax has
hardened, remove the rubber bands, and then carefully lift one half of the
mold away from the candle. Then stand the candle upright and peel the
other mold half away from the candle. You should have a perfect reproduction of the original master pattern. If some wax has seeped a bit into the
seams and formed a parting line, gently scrape it away with a knife.

Kinds of Mold Materials for Mold-Making

TYPE OF MATERIAL	APPLICA- TION PROBLEMS	FLEXI- BILITY- RIGIDITY	LIFE OF MOLD	COST FACTORS
Ceramic Clay	open molds and one-time coil or slab forms	plastic and moldable	one time for coil and slab, three or four castings for open forms	inexpensive when used only to make a proto-type or master pattern
Epoxy	a two-part sys-tem that re-quires adequate ventilation and measuring	rigid two-part molds necessary (pours as a liquid)	long life, good detail	initial material expensive but long life justi-fies cost; a pro-fessional ma-terial
Plaster Bandage	relatively easy, requires meticu-lous application of plaster strips	rigid, two parts necessary	small number of castings, limited life	inexpensive, good for experi-mental use but not practical for repeated cast-ings
Plaster of Paris	open molds very easy; two-part molds take longer, but not difficult; release agents impor-tant	rigid open mold —one-part; closed mold— two-part (pours as heavy liquid)	medium amount depending upon care taken of mold	inexpensive; practical for limited com-mercial pro-duction
RTV Silicone Molding Rubber	a two-part sys-tem that re-quires accurate measuring and proper mixing	semiflexible (pours as a liquid); one- and two-part molds possible	long life, excel-lent detail	initial material expensive, but long life justifies cost; a profes-sional material
Stretchy Adrub	a two-part sys-tem that re-quires accurate measuring and proper mixing; easy to apply	flexible	medium life	moderate cost

6

Unusual Candles From Unusual Techniques

MOST OF THE FUN in candlemaking that comes after making one's first successful candles is creating unique, personal, and beautiful candle forms or designs that you have developed—your own expressions in candle design.

The candles described in this chapter extend the range of possibility from standard good shapes to that of the unusual. Some candles "make it" because of internal interest, the treatments in pouring and adding to the wax aspects that produce interesting effects. A second variation is on a shell and hurricane-forming principle, and a third variation distinguishes unique candles because of their shape.

Exciting ideas can come from studying these possibilities. This does not mean that a candle has to have some gimmick in its process to distinguish it. A candle can be simple, essential, and yet distinguished.

Internal Variations Make the Candle

Some essential concepts are involved here. These are candle happenings—changing angles of pouring, depth and colors of pourings, surface texture, internal textures and patterns, outside layers different from inside colors, and so on. These variations go beyond surface decoration and are built into the structure of the candles themselves to become an integrated whole.

HURRICANE CANDLE-
REFILL CONCEPT

Materials

candle mold
two colors
melted wax
pouring pitchers
knife
wicking
silicone release spray

About the Process

Pouring a color of wax into a mold, allowing a shell to form, and then pouring out the remaining wax is called the hurricane candle concept. In some cases, with some decorations, the shell itself can be used, but in this case the making of a hurricane shell is the first step in decorative possibilities.

Spray release into your mold. String your wick. Then pour the color of the higher melting point wax you want for the outside of your candle. Allow the wax to harden until a shell of ⅛–¼" forms and pour out the remaining wax. Allow the shell to cool completely and remove it from the mold. Then carve shapes into the shell.

Replace the hurricane shell in the mold. Make certain that the candle seam is properly aligned, and rethread the wick through the mold's wick hole.

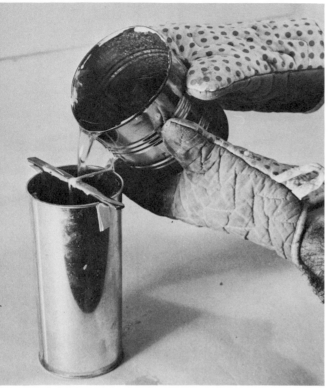

Pour a second color of a lower melting point wax into the hurricane shell and refill the wick cavity as usual.

The second color of the pouring fills the carved cavities in the hurricane shell. If you pour different colored layers, the polka dots will be different colors.

POURING LAYERS

About the Process

Floss Perisho varies her pourings so that she has different bands of contrasting and blending color in horizontal stripes. A variation on the theme is to set the mold on an angle and pour different layers at different angles. This produces diagonal color patterns.

Setting the candle mold on an angle and allowing each layer to harden before the next pouring produces diagonal striations.

Floss Perisho's horizontal striped candles. The big one is 14″ high.

CORRUGATED TEXTURE

Materials

  candle mold
  silicone release
  scissors
  corrugated paper
  adhesive tape
  colored wax

About the Process

Corrugation is a texture that is but one approach—bristol board can be scored, shaped, and inserted into the mold to create variations of surface angles as well.

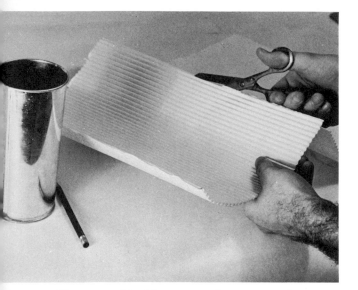

Fit your mold with corrugated paper exactly fitting from edge to edge. Tape the seam with very sticky adhesive tape.

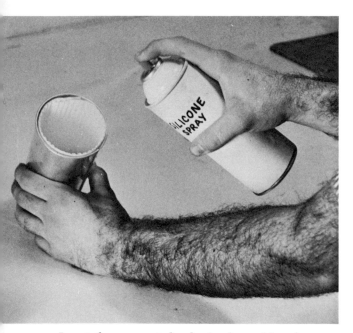

Insert the corrugated tube in the mold and spray well with silicone. Insert your wick. Pour a shallow layer of high melting point wax into the base so that it seals the corrugated tube to the base of the mold. When the floor of wax hardens, pour a lower melting point cooler wax (no more than 160° F.) into the mold.

Treat the candle in the usual way. When cool, remove the candle and peel away the corrugated paper carefully. If you peel it away too fast, some of the projections of wax will peel away with it, as shown here.

Spray the mold. String your wick. Stuff the mold very full with torn pieces of aluminum or plastic foil.

Fill the mold with wax at a very high temperature (240° F.). Tap the sides of the mold to release entrapped air.

FOIL CANDLES

Materials

metallic foil—gold/silver
candle mold
colored wax
wicking
mold release

About the Process

There are two approaches here. You can place a narrow candle in the center of your mold and then add foil, or you can completely stuff the mold with foil. The amount, placement of the foil, and the color of the wax will produce variations on the theme.

This foil treatment is restrained and random in effect.

A hexagonal candle with foil kept out of the corners. The candle is by Hallmark.

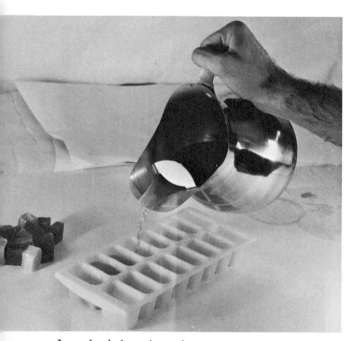

In polyethylene ice cube trays, cast a large amount of different colored cubes. These chunks can also be purchased in candle supply stores and through catalogs.

CHUNK OR CUBE CANDLE

Materials

>   ice cube trays—polyethylene is best
>   different colors of wax
>   mold release
>   wicking
>   mold
>   more wax for final pouring
>   propane torch
>   aluminum tin
>   a base candle (optional)

About the Process

Cubes of wax create beautiful random effects in multicolors. The candle surface can vary depending upon the amount of cubes used and whether you use heat to melt down the surface as a final step.

Using a candle as a core is optional. If you do, place the candle in the center of your mold and fill the mold with assorted chunks —different colors, sizes, and angles. Pour a bit of wax in the base to fix the core candle.

Fill the mold with wax (175° F.) to the top. Tap the sides of your mold to release entrapped air and fill again with more wax.

When cool, release the candle from the mold. If it looks like this, there were not enough chunks added and air was also entrapped.

Place the candle in a dish to catch wax, and, with a propane torch, starting at the top, melt away the outer coating of wax until chunks are clearly revealed.

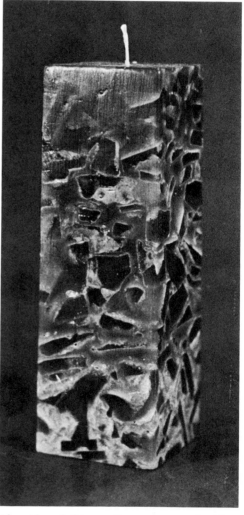

This candle is 9″ in diameter and filled with honey-type colors.

The sides of this candle were scraped with a knife. No propane torch was used.

ICE CANDLE

Materials

ice
ice pick
candle mold
duck tape to attach the wick
mold release
candle for center
clear wax
dipping tube
paper toweling

About the Process

Irregular cavities and shapes are produced by spaces held by ice when hot wax is poured over ice chunks. Colors of wax and inner candles can vary as well as the size of the ice chunks and slight variations in the pouring temperature of the wax. All of this can produce differences in the surface quality of the candle.

Chop ice or cubes into small irregular chunks about 1″ square.

After spraying the mold with release, Betty Thomforde has placed a blue candle in the center of the larger mold and taped the wick to the base with duck tape. She then poured three scoopfuls of hot wax into the mold so it would stand up and hold the candle in place.

Mrs. Thomforde then threw in three ice cubes to help set the wax and continued packing the mold with ice cubes until it was filled to the top.

After filling the mold with ice, she placed her hand over the mouth of the mold and emptied it of water. Otherwise, if water remains at the bottom of the mold, there will be a break in the wax at that point.

Working quickly, she poured hot wax over the ice until the mold was filled with wax. After the wax had set up, Betty Thomforde poured out as much water as possible and then let the candle fall out of the mold.

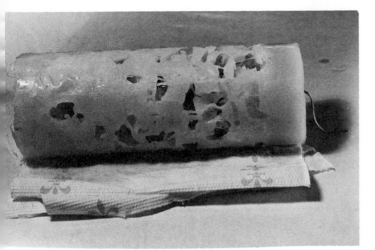

The wet candle was allowed to drain on paper towels.

The next day, when the candle was dry, it was dipped into hot wax.

The amount of dipping and the heat of the dipping wax determines whether the edges remain crisp and angular or are rounded and soft as in this version of Betty Thomforde's candle.

All materials are gathered together.

CUPCAKE CANDLE

Materials

cupcake tins
different colored waxes
milk carton
wick
scissors
duck tape to affix the wick
propane torch
knife

About the Process

Eric and Barbara Zelman designed this candle as a variation on the chunk candle concept. The result, however, is very different and very attractive. Different stacking of the "cupcake" units will produce variations in the result.

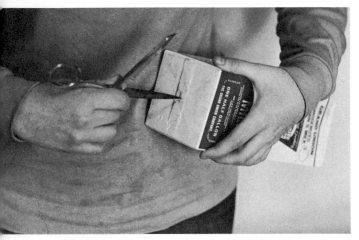

A milk carton is pierced to accommodate the wick.

Wicking is strung through the carton . . .

. . . and cut with enough wire wick left to . . .

. . . roll into a coil.

Duck tape is placed over the wire wick coil and securely fastened.

Alternating cupcake pieces are stacked in a spiraling way around the wick while the wick is pulled taut.

Shell paraffin, with 10 percent stearic acid, heated to 212° F., is poured over the cupcakes until the carton is full of wax.

The wick is anchored.

136

In three to five hours the candle has cooled, the carton is peeled away, the wick is unstuck, and the candle is removed.

Then Barbara Zelman melts away surface wax with a propane torch.

The melting operation continues until the cupcakes are revealed.

Excess wax is trimmed from the base.

Barbara and Eric Zelman's candle is about
10″ tall.

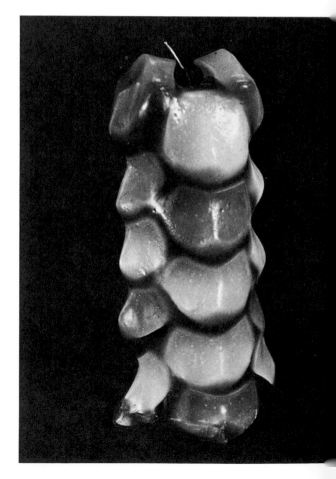

138

SHELL TYPES

Sometimes shells of wax are used with candle centers or as hurricane lamps. Two concepts are used to make wax shell forms. One is to pour wax into a mold, let it set, and then pour out the unhardened portion; the other is to dip a flexible object, such as a balloon, into the wax and then deflate or compress the flexible form and remove it to leave a shell. Very large, lightweight candle forms can be made this way, giving the appearance of solidity without a concentration of wax.

Spray your mold with release. Balance it for pouring. Fill your mold with wax. Allow it to stand until the shell is thick enough (¼"–½").

Cut away the center of the skin that formed.

Pour back the excess wax. Repeat the operation for the second half of the candle. Make a groove in both to accommodate a taper. Seal the taper in place with a heating pen or with hot wax. Heat and level both halves on a heated cookie sheet and immediately join them together.

Seal the edges by running a heating pen down the sides, and the candle is completed. As the candle burns down into the hollow of the candle it causes the shell to glow.

SHELL HALVES AND HURRICANE TYPES

Materials

open mold
knife
colored wax
thin taper

About the Process

The "hurricane" technique of making a shell is simple. Variations are possible in any size, and shells can be joined if they are symmetrical.

Cast two parts as a shell. Level both on a heated cookie sheet.

Fill hollows with wax.

Cut a groove for the wicking and put the wick in place allowing one end to protrude.

Coat the two flat surfaces quickly with hot wax and immediately press the two halves together firmly making certain that the edges meet. Let the candle harden. Trim away any excess wax or roll the edge on the heated sheet and at the same time melt a flat section in the bottom of the candle for standing.

This is a beautiful small candle that burns well.

Shell halves can be threaded onto a taper and stacked in different patterns by using hot wax to stick halves together. A final dipping in hot wax will fill seams and provide an overall finish.

142

Make a shell of wax of at least 140° F. melting point—the higher the better. Allow the walls to be at least ¼" thick. Remove the shell when cool. Draw your picture to fit the hurricane shell and, with a pencil point, trace the design onto the wax.

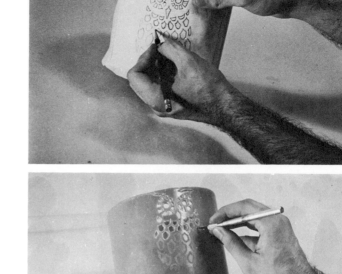

With a sharp knife carve out your shapes so that it looks like a stencil. Support your form so that it does not crack.

Clean crumbs of wax away with a stiff brush and smooth the edges with a quick pass of the flame from a propane torch.

Put a bit of water on the bottom of the hurricane shell to keep the votive from melting the wax as it burns down to the bottom. Then place a votive candle into the hurricane shell and enjoy the light flickering through your design.

This candle is made by a hurricane-type pouring in a fancy deeply carved mold to produce a ready-made pierced form without the need to carve.

This is a commercially made candle by Hallmark.

BALLOON TYPES

Materials

> balloons
> water
> hot colored wax
> knife or heating pen
> votive

About the Process

This is a very easy technique that is a lot of fun. Good results are easy to attain. Four variations on this theme are shown, but more are possible. Size is of no import either. The bigger your balloon and the more water you use, the bigger your wax shell will be. You can dip the balloon partially into the wax to obtain cuplike forms, or all the way to produce a wax ball.

To make a balloon mold, first make a water balloon. Stretch the mouth of your balloon around the water faucet and hold it firmly in place. Then turn on tepid water, and under this pressure fill your balloon to the desired circumference. (Water is more desirable than air because water helps to congeal the wax. Hot wax would expand the air in your balloon and possibly cause it to burst.) When you have your balloon mold, dip it into the hot wax (160° F.) as many times as needed until you reach the desired thickness.

Even though the balloon mold looks elliptical when held, as soon as it is dipped the shape somehow becomes spherical. Open the balloon and pour out the water and remove it from your shell.

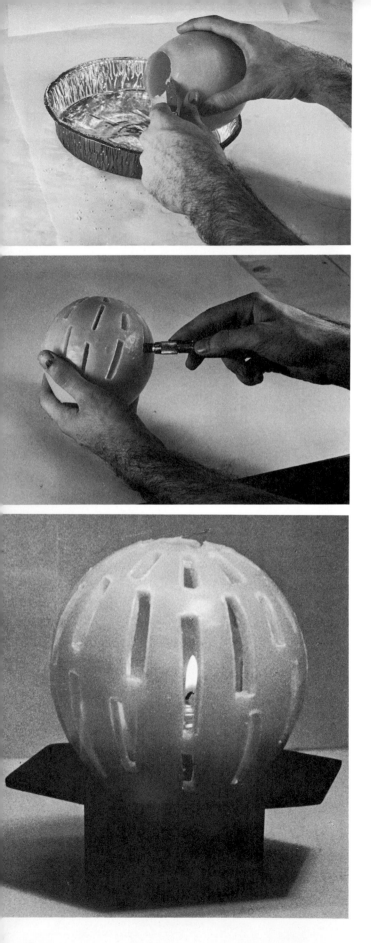

Trim the shell with a knife while the wax is still slightly warm, but take care not to apply too much pressure.

Carve your designs into the wax with a sharp knife.

Place the wax ball shell over your votive candle. This one is orange and glows like a lighted pumpkin.

146

Prepare your water balloon. The temperature of the wax should be about 160° F.

Dip the water balloon into the hot wax as many times as needed to obtain the thickness you wish. When cool, remove the balloon mold.

Shells can be cut into petal forms.

The petal forms can be joined with either hot wax or a heating pen.

147

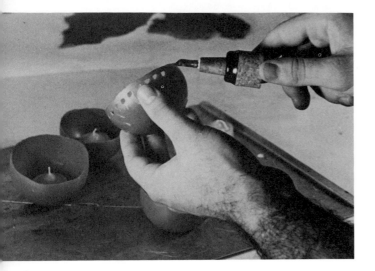

Or floating candle forms can be made by trimming the edge of the shell and piercing decorative patterns with either a knife or a heating pen. Just place a votive candle in the shell—no permanent attachment is necessary.

Floating votive candles in a wax shell can grace a punch bowl or act as a centerpiece.

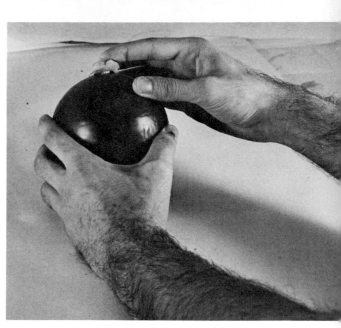

After making shells around water balloons, pierce a hole in the top of the shell with a hot ice pick or knitting needle.

Then thread your wick through the hole and seal the hole with plastic putty (Mortite).

Support the shell and center the wick. Then, with a low melting point wax no hotter than 130° F., start to fill the wax shell. Fill the shell in stages— a bit at a time—so that the heat from the wax does not build up and deform the shell.

When the shells have been filled and are cool, trim away the excess wax.

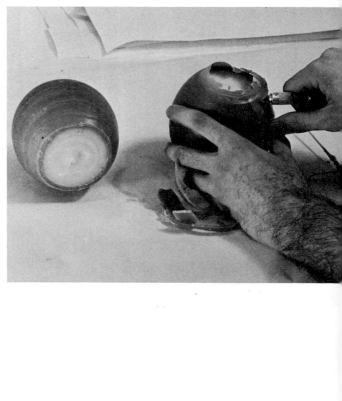

These candles owe their attractive texture to a chemical reaction as hot wax of a different melting point filled the shells. The outside covering is brown, and the candle filling is yellow.

This is a bomb from Barcelona. Very large— a 15″ diameter—and very lightweight, because it is just a shell with a candle running through it. Some of the candles in shell forms are spring-loaded so that they continue to pop up as they burn.

THE CANDLE IS ITS SHAPE

These candles are made essentially without a mold. The *process* is what determines shape, whether pouring wax into sand, layering sheets of wax, braiding, using sheets for making flower forms, or using beeswax varieties and water to shape wax into weird forms. Creative possibilities take unusual directions because there are not the constrictions of the mold used or of traditional conventions. Possibility is unlimited and results are very unusual indeed.

SAND CAST CANDLES

Materials

> sand
> spoon, knife, or tongue depressors
> wick
> hot colored wax
> container for sand
> water

For polyester-sand varieties

> polyester resin
> MEK (methyl ethyl ketone) peroxide
>   catalyst

About the Process

Early people who had no metal or wooden molds used form-giving materials that were available to them. For some candles, clay was scooped out and wax was poured into its cavity; for those living along sandy shores moist sand was used to form candles.

The sand-casting process is very simple. In slightly moistened sand, form your shape in the negative. Set your wick in place by using a wick holder and wire wick, or, after pouring the wax, tie the wick to a weight such as a washer and drop the wick into the wax. The heat of the wax being poured makes a difference as to how much sand sticks to the candle part. Very hot wax (at least 300°F.) will penetrate into the wet sand more and provide a thicker sand shell—less water in the sand will provide the same result. If little sand is desired, then use more water in the sand and a cooler pouring temperature for the wax.

Variations on this theme are many. Polyester resin mixed with 40–50 percent sand can be built around a candle form to provide a permanent shell that can be refilled with wax after use.

Also, bentonite, a white, low micron, massive, claylike filler that does not swell when wet, helps to give a very strong almost cementlike quality to sand cast candles. It is a very good filler to use with sand when doing production sand casting in molds that were made from original sand cast pieces.

Sand and bentonite can be mixed with polymer emulsions such as acrylic or copolymers of acrylic and polyvinyl chloride, enough to wet down the sand so that it can be packed into a mold as a shell and provide what really becomes a shell container (when cured or hard) into which wax is poured. These copolymer emulsions (Elmer's Glue works, too), which are water soluble, act as an adhesive that glues sand particles together and will not separate from moist sand, if used in a mold. Another variation, therefore, is to proceed as usual in making a sand cast candle, except after forming your shape in the sand, coat the inside of the cavity with one of these polymer emulsions, mixing it into the sand a bit. Allow this to harden before pouring your wax. The sandy outer surface will become a hard shell.

All these sand forms look best as organic shapes, not contrived into geometric forms or fancy carvings.

In a container of sand, mix sand with enough water to make the sand moldable.

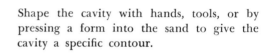

Shape the cavity with hands, tools, or by pressing a form into the sand to give the cavity a specific contour.

Add your wick.

Pour very hot wax into the cavity. Tend to the cavity that forms around the wick in the usual way by piercing it and refilling with wax.

When the wax has hardened, scoop the form out of the sand.

Lift the candle out by the wick.

Polyester resin, mixed in proper proportions (according to instructions) with its catalyst, methyl ethyl ketone peroxide, is then mixed with no more than 50 percent sand. This should become a thixotropic mixture that will not drain off of inclined surfaces. Place your candle upside down on waxed paper and mold the sand with a tongue depressor around your sand cast candle.

The legs were cut away from the original sand cast candle because they made a clumsy-looking shape. The original sand cast candle was formed by Kenneth Hamilton.

These are production made "sand cast" candles that use different fillers and additives. The striations in the surface are originally naturally formed because that particular Florida beach (New Smyrna) has layers of Cocina shell and sand that have been compacted in various densities by the tides. When the sand additive is added it absorbs more deeply into some striations than into others, causing the beautiful natural-looking texture. *Courtesy Bill Stone of Stone Candles*

This gang-form of five candles was formed at the same striated sand beach. The sand surface is not loose and gritty, but very hard and compact, almost the density of cement. *Courtesy Bill Stone of Stone Candles*

A side view. *Courtesy Bill Stone of Stone Candles*

Stack your wax sheets and then soften them with a propane torch or another heat source so that the sheets can be folded into a basic log shape.

LAYERED CANDLES

Materials

> sheets of wax in various colors
> a cookie sheet
> an aluminum tin
> wicks
> propane torch

About the Process

There is a random effect to these candles that makes every step in their creation a surprise. The flame of the propane torch becomes a sculpturing instrument that reveals layers of wax and molds the outside form. The combination of colors and the way the sheets of wax are folded will create different variations. Wax sheets can be poured weeks in advance and stored between waxed paper until you have enough colors. In the process of forming your shape the "log" looks terrible, but do not despair; keep sculpting until colors and shapes are revealed.

When working with a propane torch keep your room well ventilated to draw off fumes from the wax. Never keep your propane torch in one spot too long; otherwise, if the wax gets too hot, it may ignite. Keep baking soda nearby to dust any flames that may form.

With a propane torch sculpt the surface so that the flame of the torch reveals various layers and creates a pleasing contour. After you have achieved the form, determine the center and, with a heated knitting needle, make a wick hole and insert your wicking.

These layered candles are not unlike natural forms such as the petrified wood shape on the right.

This layered paraffin candle was made of thicker layers of wax that were rolled, jelly roll fashion, into this form.

BRAIDED CANDLES

Materials

   pan
   hot colored wax
   wick

About the Process

Wax-coated wicks are thin candles. When
soft, they can be braided, like string,
macramé fashion into various shapes.

The technique shown here was very easy
to do. Fancy macramé knotting is possible and could form very interesting
patterns.

The temperature of wax is critical
when dipping or pulling wicking
through wax. Wax at 100°F. leaves the
greatest amount of wax on the wick,
200°F. leaves less wax on the wick, and
wax at 250°F. melts the previous wax
layers off the wick leaving less on than
before. This holds true for dipping
candles in wax as well.

Cut your square braided cotton wicking to
the desired length. Pull the wicking through
wax at about 150° F. Allow a few seconds
for layers to cool.

For this design, three strips of the same
length are needed. Anchor the top end, and,
while the waxed wicks are still warm and
malleable, twist them into a braided shape.

These candles have a definite charm. Because
three wicks are burning together the flame is
very large.

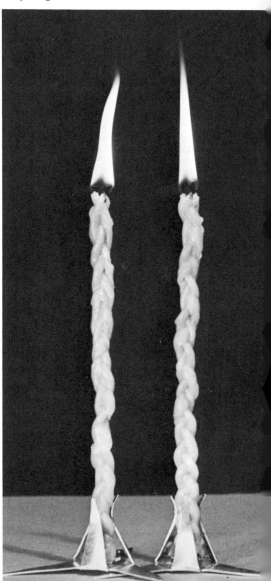

FLOWER CANDLES

Materials

> sheets of wax—mostly beeswax
> knife
> egg shaped candle
> pinking shears (optional)
> thin wire

About the Process

Any flower can be made using the basic technique illustrated here. Betty Thomforde's rose candle can become a pansy, lily, gladiola, or any soft petaled flower.

Prepared beeswax sheets can be used, or sheets of wax containing at least 30–50 percent beeswax can be poured and kept pliable while working. Mrs. Thomforde pours her sheet of wax on plate glass that is set into a box (edges of the glass are sealed). The box contains four electric light bulbs that are shielded between bulb and glass with aluminum foil the thickness of a pie tin. The bulbs permit the wax to harden only to working consistency—keeping the glass just warm enough to maintain the wax sheet soft enough for shaping.

Pour a low melting point wax that consists of at least ⅓ beeswax into a sheet of about ¼₆″ thickness.

Start with an egg shape around which petals are layered. Cut a rose petal with a knife.

Smooth out and thin the edges of the petal. Cut three petals to cover the egg and press them to the egg after warming the egg in your hands.

Betty Thomforde keeps cutting petals, thinning edges, and shaping them. Cut petals larger and larger and more oval shaped as you get to the outside petals. As you go along, pull out the petals more and more until you reach the bottom largest petals. Pull away excess wax at the base so the flower does not get too bulky. After all petals are in place, dip the flower into cold water.

Cut leaf shapes from a wax sheet. Lightly score the veins of the leaf with your fingernail or some dull-pointed object.

With pinking shears trim the edge of your leaf.

160

Smooth and thin out the edge by pressing it between your fingers.

Press very thin wire into the underside of the leaf and shape the leaf in a curve before sticking the bottom into the base of the rose candle.

Betty Thomforde's rose candle. A variation of this can be to form a rose or another flower at the base of a taper.

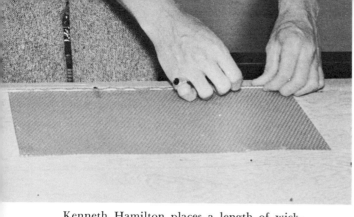

Kenneth Hamilton places a length of wicking on the edge of a honeycomb beeswax sheet. He folds the edge over the wick on the plywood table and crimps the edge so that it hugs the wick snugly.

This candle requires three 8½″ x 16″ sheets, one rolled into the next. The sheets are rolled tightly; before the end of one sheet is reached he overlaps it with another sheet until all three sheets are used.

Four other sheets of different colors are cut in thirds lengthwise.

BEESWAX RAINBOW SWIRL CANDLES

Materials

> *beeswax honeycomb sheets in assorted colors*
> *wicking*
> *knife*

About the Process

Tightly coiled beeswax is an easy candle to make. Beeswax in honeycombed sheets can be rolled into very thick, thin, tall, short shapes. The tops of the candles can be sealed by rolling the candle top on a heated cookie sheet.

Variations can be created by adding coils and shapes to a basic shape. These can be applied vertically, diagonally, horizontally, and in various overall designs.

Honeycomb beeswax sheets can be made from slices of natural honeycomb, or more usually are manufactured of a beeswax consistency wax in a honeycomb pattern—complete with the scent of beeswax.

Each edge is bent over the edge of the plywood table and then each of these twelve pieces is rolled tightly.

Then each roll is curved slightly around the candle—seams inward. They are pressed on lightly at first, just in case an adjustment in spacing is required later. Then, after a progression of spiraled colors is added, the entire candle is squeezed firmly to adhere all the parts. The edges are pressed to even out projections.

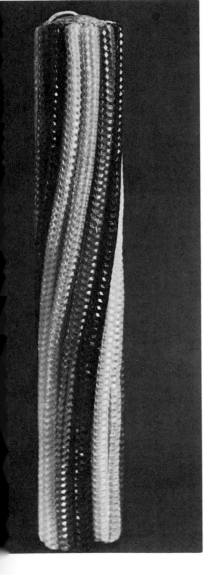

These are different size variations of natural rolled beeswax honeycomb candles.

Kenneth Hamilton of Bayonne, New Jersey, designed this rainbow spiral beeswax honeycomb candle. It is 16" tall.

WAX FANTASY CANDLES

Materials

> cold to tepid water
> water container—broad and deep
> melted wax
> candle for center
> container for the candle

About the Process

Each piece is different. No two can be alike. The consistency of your wax (soft,

hard, high or low melting point), the temperature of the water, the depth and breadth of the container, the speed of dunking, the amount of wax, and the shape of the container holding the wax all determine what kind of weird wax pattern will result. These are variables worth experimenting with when making these fantasy candles.

By blocking off areas in your container and pouring a different color of wax in each, other strange combinations result. There is no end to possibilities.

Water patterns shape the molten wax as a pan of hot wax is submerged in water. Two hands should be used for submerging the container. One of many fantastic shapes.

Place a candle, a small, medium, or tall taper, into your container and fix it in place with a bit of wax that you allow to harden.

Fill the container with 165° F. wax at least 1½–2″ high, and with two hands immediately submerge the container in cool water. (Wear rubber gloves to keep hot wax from stinging your hands. If you don't, the wax will not cause a burn at that temperature.) Keep the wax submerged until all wax has risen and the wax is cool.

Lift out and drain off.

Two varieties made in disposable clear styrene cups. These are to be used as individual favors on a table setting.

Use of a tall taper and a pot pie tin to hold the wax. The pot pie tin has been removed. The base needs scraping and leveling.

Use of a medium sized taper in a bowl with a 5″ diameter and 1½″ depth. Wax fantasy and candle are the same color.

MISCELLANEOUS

The following two candle types do not fit neatly into any category. One is an aggregate which uses two molds and then is joined. The other receives its random shape by the way wicking is wrapped around a basic form and burns, melting grooves around the candle. It is a process—because of the interesting, ever-changing patterns that result as the wicking burns.

AGGREGATES

Mushroom aggregate candle. Two mold shapes were selected and sprayed with silicone release before wax was poured.

After the forms cooled and were released from their molds, the base was leveled in a heated tin.

Then the top of the cone was heated and pressed immediately to the mushroom cap. Some hot wax was poured onto the underside.

Wax was dripped on for trimming and to add a variation in color. Then, instead of stringing a wick through the two pieces, a key-wick was used.

This is one variety of mushroom and one variety of the many possibilities with aggregates. Here are some more possibilities. Try combining blocks (using individual juice cartons as molds) to make a train. Several different sized balls form rabbits, bears, beavers, and other animals. Sheeting can be shaped for ears. Thin tapers around a ball can form a sunburst. Christmas angels may be created from a cone, ball, and sheet of wax for wings.

OUTSIDE WICK

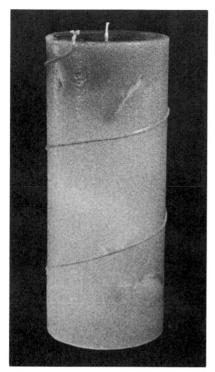

A block candle is wrapped with wire wicking in a spiral pattern. The wick is attached with melted wax.

Note that the wick is burning and causing the candle to melt. (The flame of the second wick is visible on the upper left of the candle.) Chunks that were cast into the mold are revealed. Watching the shape change continuously is the most interesting part of this candle.

The final candle with its amorphous contours. Changing the way the wick is wrapped will produce variations in shape.

A GALLERY OF BEAUTIFUL CANDLE FORMS

Variations in shape, some very subtle, internal differences in color, decorative treatment of surfaces, and chemical treatment of the wax to produce chemical changes all are employed to create individual and handsome candle forms. Some of the departures taken by candle designers are very slight, others are more dramatic; all are beautiful.

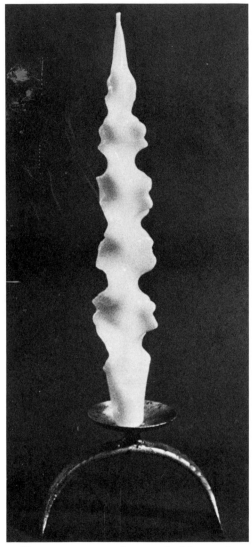

You can sense a finger pinching and fluting the edges of a softened taper. The original may have been made this way. A mold was made from the prototype candle. Origin—Barcelona, Spain.

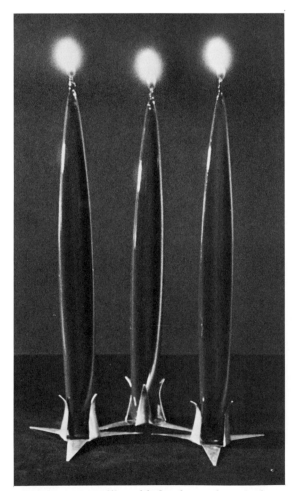

The taper curves like a blade of grass from its base. Origin—Barcelona, Spain.

A pitchfork evolves into a taper candle form. Origin—Scandinavia.

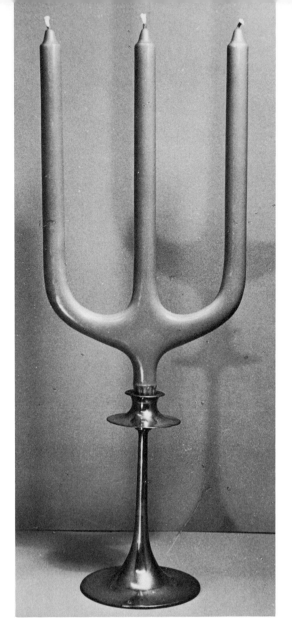

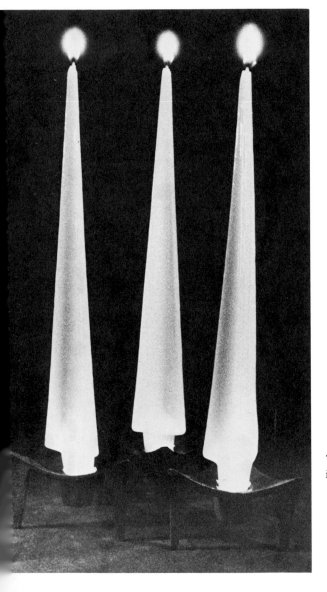

Triangular ribs project from an angular concavity in this triangular form. Origin—Spain.

Lee Weber's simple shapes in appealing proportions have a sculptural purity of line. *Courtesy Lee Weber*

Mineral oil in cool pure paraffin made for this appealing texture.

Like the turned wooden form on the right, these are two variations in shape that make for very attractive candles.

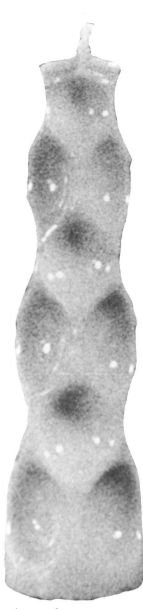

A cross between a taper and a molded block candle, this thin form with concave depressions is as freestanding as a block candle. Origin—Barcelona, Spain.

Two cones were joined to create a variation on an hourglass concept. Origin—Flair Candles.

Banded colors in subtle variations and well thought out
widths of stripes characterize
this suspended candle.

Wax rolled jelly roll fashion, sliced and attached like shells to a block candle marks
this design. As the candle burns, the surface
will be illuminated by the interior flame.

A flower carved and filled decorates this block candle. It has a pitted texture. It is pleasing to look at and has a blueberry scent.

A milk glass form was made into a mold. A candle was cast in two colors—exterior and interior color. When burning, the two tones will illuminate in translucent and transparent patterns.

Fluted and round, these almost porcelain glossy candles come in gay colors. Note that the exact sameness of the two suggests that a mold was used to form these. Origin—Barcelona, Spain.

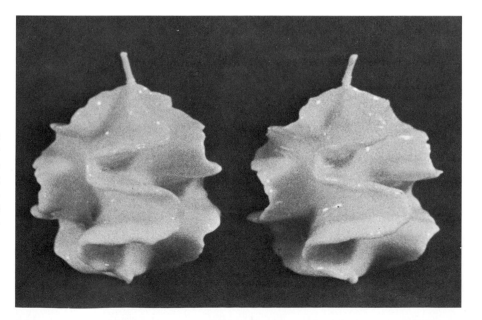

7

The Candleholder
Is the Candle

FOR SOME CANDLES, the shape they have is integrated with their container, which, like the turtle shell and turtle, stays with it as a housing. For other candles to be considered here, the candleholder makes the candle and in a way gives the candle a new form and an attractiveness that it did not have before. This is the case with votive candles and similar "cheap" mass-produced small candles.

There are all sorts of possibilities not included in the illustrations here. For example, antique dishes, beautiful earthenware forms, old glasses, the odd glass, or a piece of stoneware left from a set that once existed are among some of the containers that can be filled with wax and enjoyed as candles. Found objects such as flowerpots, odd metal shapes, glass bottles in odd shapes can also make attractive candle forms. Chunk glass arranged in a brandy glass around a votive candle reflects candlelight with flickering projections of color. Stained-glass forms can also be used as candle containers. In fact, if you look around the house, the attic, or basement, or take a walk in the woods, you will find any number of potential containers. Look for the unexpected. Discovering a new container form for a candle often can bring more satisfaction than copying something that has been done countless times.

FILLING OF A CANDLE CONTAINER

Materials

candle container
wicking and wick tabs or holders
hot wax and color
various other tools for special effects

About the Process

Filling containers is very simple. The biggest problem is fixing the wick tab, a small square metal attachment to hold the wick. The wick tab or holder has its corners bent upward so that when the candle hardens the wick will become fixed at the base. All votive candles have wick tabs.

Attach your wick to a tab, and pour a bit of wax to fix the wick and tab to the container's base. Let this harden. Straighten and center the wick so it does not swim around when the wax is poured.

Make certain that your container is warm if it is glass, and pour the rest of your wax at just the melting point (whatever it may be) so that the glass will not crack from the heat of the wax.

This candle, a "pudding dessert," was poured in flavorful layers; each time a layer hardened another layer was poured. Take care not to pour wax down the container sides, but in true center if you wish a distinct layer effect. After the wick hollow was filled, wax was whipped and applied.

It looks delicious enough to eat and as a candle it has a wee light—but it is a "fun" candle.

Connect your wick tab to wicking, cotton, or wire. In glass containers I use wire wicking because it is easier to straighten and burns with a smaller flame. Because the flame is hotter, you should use a smaller wick. With alligator clips or any other way, make certain that the wick stands straight and centered. Then pour a small amount of wax to set the tab. Allow this to cool and then pour the rest of your wax.

Because this container, an apothecary jar, has a lid, it becomes an excellent container for highly scented candles because the cover will help to keep the scent from dissipating.

178

This flowerpot container is great for citronella scented outdoor candles. This one has a huge flair candlewick, which is a woven bias sleeve of cotton stuffed with cotton filler. It burns with a large smoky flame—quite appropriate to keep mosquitoes away.

Rope tied into a macramé design suspends two wax-sand cast candles. Here again, the candle container is refillable.

Polyester and sand house the owl form candle. When the owl loses its head, the polyester and sand will forever be the candle container. And when the candle wax burns away, the container is refillable.

179

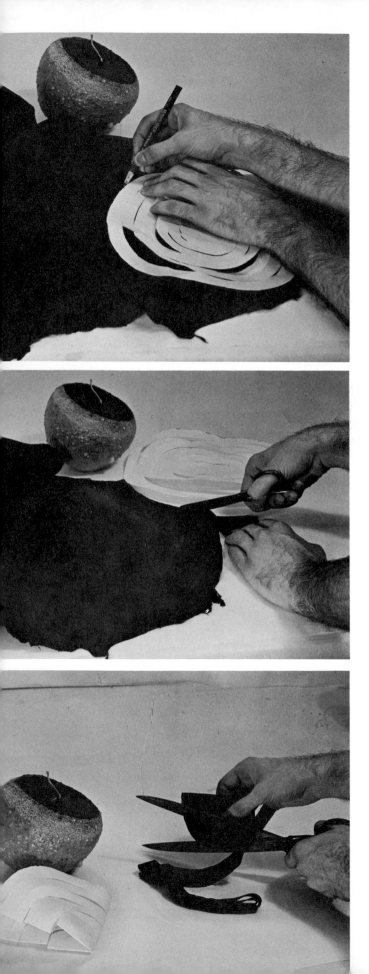

This sand cast candle needs a sling for suspension. A paper form is cut to fit. Then it is traced onto the leather.

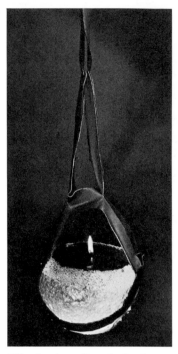

The leather sling is the housing of this candle by Betty Thomforde.

An outline of the shape is cut from the leather.

Sections are cut the same as the paper model. From alternate edges parallel curves are cut almost to the opposite edge of a circle that has been folded into a quarter segment.

180

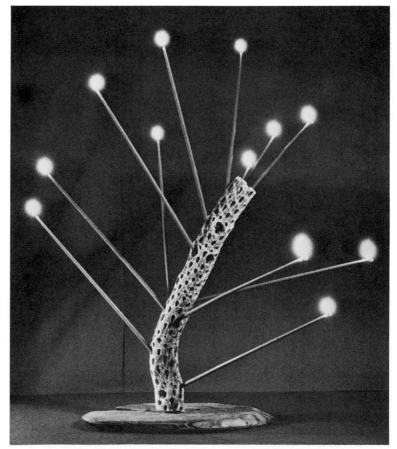

This beautiful candle, about 12″ in diameter, is its own candleholder. Twigs are used to anchor and attach leather thongs that pierce the candle at three points. The candle itself is colored by broad brushstrokes of peach and brown hot wax.

Creature candle by Donovan is its own container that sits on its plastic feet. His head has half a dozen wicks so he can burn in varying designs and amounts.

This beautiful cholla wood form was found supporting a philodendron plant. Its holes make a natural candleholder. Only thin tapers such as these can be angled so much and burn without dripping wax all over the table.

This beautiful giant driftwood hollow is gorgeous as a candle. There were many holes that had to be plugged with Mortite. The wax was poured slowly and in stages. This candle will live on and on because I'll continue to fill it.

Ordinary votive candles can become elegant lamps when supported by candle-holders such as these made of acrylic. *Courtesy Jay and Lee Newman*

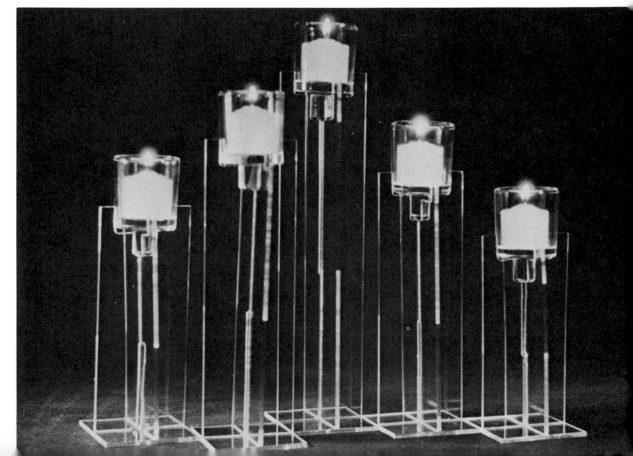

This old Spanish hand-formed sterling silver candleholder is the only means by which the beeswax rope can burn. Whereas a candle can sit in almost anything and stand with wick ready to burn, the grandfather rope needs to be strung and its coil rotated.

A cylinder formed of fused Poly-Mosaic set in leading provides a windless cover and a romantic light for some old candle. Form about 12" high. *Courtesy Jay and Lee Newman*

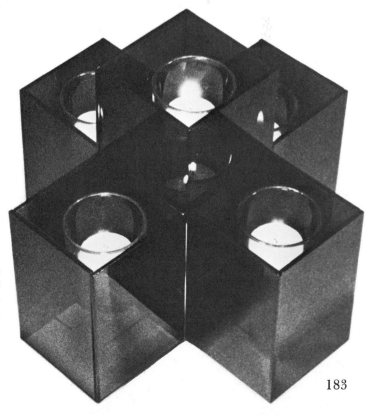

Again the votive rises to elegant heights as it rests in different levels in these smoky acrylic boxes designed by Jay and Lee Newman. *Courtesy Jay and Lee Newman*

183

How important would these 2″ candles be without this attractive brass candelabrum?

Like the mysterious face of a woman hidden by a veil, this candle presides in mystery within the smoky acrylic hurricane lamp designed by Jay and Lee Newman. *Courtesy Jay and Lee Newman*

8

The Candle Environment
Some Scenes From
a Candle's Life

WITHOUT ANY DOUBT, the candle adds interest, a focal point, drama, emphasis, romantic description to any environment. There is something peaceful and relaxing about a room where candlelight is flickering.

Candles in their habitat can be treated formally, informally, naturally, even primitively. Their props—the period of furnishing, the style of candleholder or candelabrum—play a great role in determining mode and mood. Here is where individuality goes beyond the creative making of a candle to the even more important creative arrangement of the candle. For only when the candle moves out of the studio into its environment does it live and function—to be enjoyed by all.

Use of natural materials—the straw tray (Amazonian flour sifter), a piece of driftwood, flowers, and a candle growing from the arrangement as a blade of grass—harmoniously combine to become a very inviting spot in a room.

More formal, this candelabrum supports four candles of dramatic contemporary form in a brass candle-flower container. The setting is a coffee table in a modern living room.

Another flower-candle arrangement, this time in a gold lacquer bowl. Both the flowers and the candle shine with life.

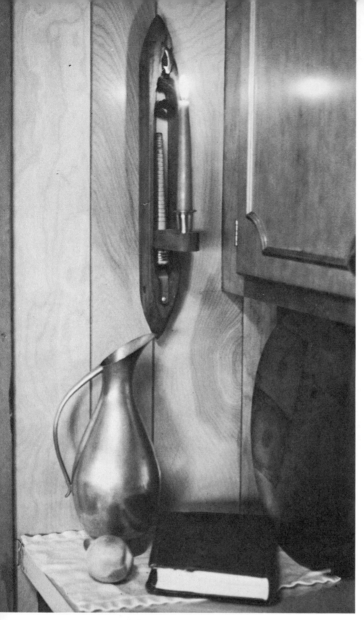

A weaver's shuttle becomes a candleholder in
this colonial setting, a corner in a breakfast
room. Textures abound—wood, pewter, linen,
leather, lacquer—all subtly illuminated by a
very simple hand dipped candle.

Pure, stark, Japanese in inspiration, these
four flat blades of beeswax are pinned in a
flower holder that is covered with polished
pebbles. Informal balance keynotes the drama
of this arrangement.

188

Donna Rosa of Oaxaca, Mexico, created this ceramic hurricane sculpture that houses a votive candle. The harmonizing tablecloth and wall hanging also come from south of the border.

These Tibetan temple torches, small and large, are propped in a flowerpot filled with pebbles. The panel behind it is a religious painting by the Wayana Indians of Surinam, South America.

189

Another scene from south of the border—the Mexican tin and copper mirror reflects a Guatemalan ceremonial embroidery whose colors are repeated in a Mexican painted ceramic tree of life candelabrum. The colors are very gay and warm. The candle shapes, small and simple, do not compete with the barrage of primitive color and pattern in this New World Spanish atmosphere.

All the forms in this arrangement are hand-made. Each of the materials used dramatizes its own qualities—the stoneware bowl and owl, the natural dyes of the Guatemalan weaving, the old bronze candleholder, and the Swedish red wax candle.

A contemporary arrangement on a coffee table. The orange candle serves as an emphasis for the copper table, bronze sculpture by Cristos Capralos, blue glass lamp, and candle dish.

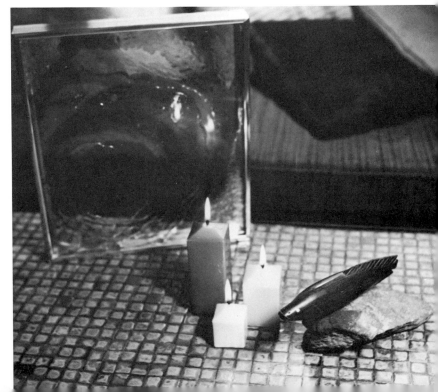

Extremely modern in color and design, this arrangement is a play of light and brilliant color.

A two-hundred-year-old bottle, a modern plate, rocks, and a shell create a beautiful blending of natural materials. The candle was forced to drip so that it could dramatize the old slave trade bottle from Surinam.

Larger candles fill the fireplace with candlelight in the colonial atmosphere of Emily McGowan's living room.

Inside and out, the candlelight beckons in this large 12″ diameter bowl shaped candle form. It is suspended by leather strips attached with twigs through the candle.

High keyed and very sophisticated, these white and clear forms relate because of color. The "puzzle" sculpture of acrylic in the background is by the author and the ice candle is by Betty Thomforde.

Here seventeen hand dipped candles in a wrought-iron candelabrum brighten and dominate this living room area—reminiscent of Spain. The picture frame is silver repoussé and it displays a Guatemalan wedding veil. The spot transmits a feeling of reverence.

Here, too, the candle is a welcoming beacon that integrates as a composition with the heather plant and West African medicine man sculpture.

Somewhat oriental in feeling, this candle relates in color and pattern to the rich variety of texture with violets, turquoises, and grays of this living room area.

196

A potpourri of styles blend in color and mood, but contrast in texture. The collage painting is by Jane Bearman.

Brass and copper antiques and a Spanish (contemporary) wooden "antique" candleholder create another focal point setting in a hallway table that has a shallow depth.

Floss Perisho of Penland, North Carolina, created these banded candles of colors that could have been inspired by the Peruvian textile and pre-Columbian ceramic sculpture.

For fun, a pop table setting of all good things to satisfy—visually that is.

A tin candleholder from Spain (Mexico has beautiful tin candle-holders as well) drama-tizes this living room arrangement. Its Span-ish candle repeats a motif similar to the candleholder and seems to become an extension of it.

Some of the over 170 different candles that have been described in this book. Which are your favorites?

Appendix

**COMMERCIAL
CANDLEMAKING**

Wicks for candles are fed into the machine from spindles on the floor below.
Courtesy Columbia Wax Products Co.

199

Hoops strung with wicks look like the romaine of the eighteenth century. Here a machine turns a few feet and the operator lowers one of the wheels into a vat containing hot wax. Each hoop is dipped thirty times before the candles are completed. The last dip is of a high melting point wax mixed with a higher amount of stearic acid to help make the candle dripless. *Courtesy Columbia Wax Products Co.*

The operator is lowering a cage of candles into its last dip of high melting point wax. *Courtesy Columbia Wax Products Co.*

The grandfather candlemaker should see this operation that in a mechanical way is so similar to his hand method. Birthday candles are being formed by running a continuous wick twelve times around two drums and through a vat of hot wax. The resulting long candle is then automatically cut up by the machine on the right. *Courtesy Columbia Wax Products Co.*

Glossary

Acrolein: A harmful by-product produced when wax decomposes because of heat.

Aging: Permitting the candle to cool to proper degree of hardness before stripping it from the mold.

Bayberry: A wax made by boiling bayberries and skimming off the wax.

Beeswax: A fatty substance that can be gathered by melting honeycombs at 145°F. To obtain two pounds of wax, bees would have to consume about fourteen times this weight in honey. The wax is originally white, but turns dark yellow with age. There is also a bee glue called propolis that bees gather from certain trees that is a resinous cement that they use to mend their honeycombs.

Blanket Mold: A mold of flexible material, usually rubber or plasticlike rubber, that entirely covers the object, except for an opening at one end.

Block Candle: A candle that is freestanding and may or may not be entirely consumed by its flame.

Bobeche: A saucerlike shape at the base of the candle on the candleholder supposedly to catch wax drippings.

Butting: Trimming excess wax from the top of a candle after it has cooled.

Cascading or *Foliating:* A special wax "dripping" process that produces billowing wings of wax when the candle is burned.

Casting: The process of pouring the melted wax into a mold.

Cave-in: A collapsing process that sometimes occurs when candles have not been properly opened, thus permitting air pockets to form.

Cetyl Alcohol: An additive that lowers the melting point of wax causing it to be softer and more malleable and produce a large flame.

Chandler: From *chandelle* candle + *ier*—one who makes and sells candles; a trader in supplies.

Decoupage: Decorating with the use of paper cutouts.

Drop Wax: A collection of remnants and leftovers of candles and drippings.

Dye: Coloring material used in candlemaking exclusively; comes in powders, liquids, and solids.

Elvax: An ethylene/vinyl acetate copolymer that when added (20 percent) makes wax harder and more glossy.

Encaustic: From the Greek "burnt in," which is melting wax color onto a background.

Foliating: See Cascading.

Frosting: Whipped or beaten wax, used extensively in decorating candles.

Green Soap: A soft soap made of potash, linseed oil, and alcohol.

Guttering: Excessive dripping of wax which smothers the flame.

Hurricane Candle: Made by pouring a color of wax into a mold, allowing a shell to form and then pouring out the remaining wax.

Impasto: A particularly thick and heavy application of a color-bearing medium.

Key-Wick: A commercial name for a small cone-shaped carbonlike material that lights and then consumes the wax that melts around it in a pool.

Master Pattern: The original form from which a mold is made.

MEK Peroxide: Methyl ethyl ketone used as one of the catalysts for polyester resin.

Modeling Wax: An equal mixture of bleached beeswax and paraffin.

Mold: Any container or receptacle used to form a candle. Molds may be made of glass, metal, plaster, plastic, rubber, cardboard, wood, or any other substance that will hold heated wax.

Molding Wax: A combination of paraffin, stearine, and beeswax, or beeswax and Venice Turpentine, or just beeswax.

Mottling Oil: A mineral oil or vegetable oil material that causes some disintegration of paraffin and therefore is evidenced in a mottled effect in the wax.

Oiling: Use of peanut or vegetable oil as an aid to candle removal from some molds.

Opening: The process of puncturing the hardened upper shell of a candle around the wick during the cooling process for the purpose of filling the interior cavity that has formed with more wax.

Paraffin: A white, translucent, waxy substance distilled from petroleum. Melting points 125°F. to 158°F.

Prototype: The original or model on which further designs are based or formed.

P.V.A.: Polyvinyl acetate, a vinyl used as an adhesive and a painting and coating medium.

Refilling: Adding additional warm wax to the center of a candle to make up for shrinkage.

R T V : Room temperature vulcanizing, when a two-part "rubber" system cures without application of heat.

Sealing Wax: A mixture of beeswax and pitch that flows when heated and is brittle when cooled.

Shrinking: Allowing natural shrinkage to occur in a candle through contraction.

Sleeve Mold: One-piece rubber molds that slip off or are rolled off of the positive.

Stearic Acid. See Stearine.

Stearine (Stearin): A form of stearic acid, a soft, opaque white, odorless solid made of natural animal and plant fats (palmitim). Melting points 122–156°F., malleable at 120°F. Stearine candles can burn well and do not bend as a result of the flame's heat.

Stringing the Mold: Placing the wick in the correct position within the mold, before casting.

Stripping: Removing a candle from the mold.

Swaddles: Rolled-up candles usually of honeycomb beeswax sheets.

Tallow: Made up of fatty animal tissue found in ox kidney suet, mutton drippings, or goat fat, and used popularly to manufacture candles. Lime was added to the melted tallow and then the tallow was cooked with vinegar for three to four hours. The odor of tallow is rancid and candles made with tallow have a greasy touch.

Taper: A slender candle of diminishing diameter that requires support in a candleholder.

Triasol: (Trichlorethylene plus ethylene dichloride), a solvent for waxes.

Trichloroethane: (Vinyl trichloride), a solvent for waxes. May be called chlorothene.

Undercuts: Indentations or projections that would lock an eventually solid casting material into a solid mold material.

Waste Mold: A mold that has to be destroyed to be removed such as glass molds for casting small spheres.

Wick Tabs or Holders: Small square metal attachments to hold the wick in place at the bottom of a candle. Votive candles have wick tabs.

Wicks: The souls of candles made of bleached and mordanted cotton yarn in various thicknesses and various weavings. The thicker the candle, the thicker the wick. Paraffin requires thin wicks, stearine needs medium wicks, with the thickest wicks reserved for beeswax candles. Wicks have a bottom and a top. Wax chandlers indicate it with a knot at the top because it is difficult to judge the difference between the top and bottom.

Bibliography

CLARK, CARL DAME. *Molding and Casting.* Baltimore: The Standard Arts Press, 1946.

COBURN, FREDERICK W. "A Group of Japanese Candlesticks," *Handicraft,* vol. 14, no. 8, November, 1911.

CRISTIANI, R. S. *A Technical Treatise on Soap and Candles.* Philadelphia: Henry Carey Baird & Co., 1881.

CUMING, J. SYER. "Pin-Lore and the Waxen Image," *The Journal of the British Archeological Association,* vol. 5, London, 1899.

DU MONCEAU, DUHAMEL. *Art du Cirer.* Paris: Académie des Sciences, 1762.

EVANS, SIR ARTHUR. *Palace of Minos.* Vol. 2, part 1. London: Macmillan Co., Ltd., 1928.

GODBOLE, N. N. *Candle Manufacture.* Benares: Benares Hindu University, 1935.

GODE, P. K. "History of Wax Candles in India 1500–1900 A.D.," *Annals of Bbandarkar Oriental Research Institute,* vol. 32, part 1–14.

Gulfwax pamphlet. "Working with Gulfwax," 1959.

HOUGH, WALTER. *Fire as an Agent in Human Culture.* Washington, D.C.: Government Printing Office, 1926.

KLENKE, WILLIAM W. *Candlemaking.* Peoria, Illinois: The Manual Arts Press, 1946.

LELAND, CHARLES GODFREY. *Useful Arts and Handicrafts.* Vol. 1. London: Dawborn & Ward, Ltd., 1900.

MORFIT, CAMPBELL. *Chemistry Applied to the Manufacture of Soap and Candles.* Philadelphia: Carey & Hart, 1847.

NEWMAN, THELMA R. *Plastics as an Art Form.* Philadelphia: Chilton Book Company, revised edition, 1969.

———. *Wax as Art Form.* South Brunswick, New Jersey: Thomas Yoseloff, 1966.

OLSEN, DON and RAY. *Modern Art of Candle Creating.* South Brunswick, New Jersey: A. S. Barnes & Co., 1963.

RADFORD, E. and M. A. *Encyclopedia of Superstition.* London: Rider & Co., 1948.

RAWSON, MARION NICHOLL. *Candle Days.* New York: The Century Collection, 1927.

ROBINS, F. W. *The Story of the Loreys.* London: Oxford University Press, 1939.

ROST, MILDRED KENNEY. *Candles of Christmas.* Published by the author, Oceanside, California, 1936.

ROY, L. M. A. *The Candle Book.* Brattleboro, Vermont: Stephen Daye Press, 1938.

RUSHFORD, EDWARD ALLEN, M.D. "Candle Molds—Types and Materials," *The Essex Institute Historical Collections,* vol. LXV, January, 1929.

Shell News. "Candles at Christmas," vol. 29, no. 12, December, 1961.

STROSE, SUSANNE. Candle-Making. New York: Sterling Publishing Co., Inc., 1970.

Sources of Supply

ADDITIVES

Colorants

Harshaw Chemical Co.
1945 E. 97th Street
Cleveland, Ohio 44106

Patent Chemicals, Inc.
335 McLean Boulevard
Paterson, New Jersey 07504

Pylam Products Co., Inc.
95–10 218th Street
Queen's Village, New York 11429

Hardeners

E. I. Du Pont de Nemours & Co., Inc.
Electrochemicals Department
350 Fifth Avenue
New York, New York 10001
  Elvax.

Premier Mfg. Co.
Denver, Colorado 80226
  Stearic acid.

F. Weber Co.
Wayne & Windrim avenues
Philadelphia, Pennsylvania 19144
  Venice Turpentine.

Scents

Berjé
43–10 23rd Street
Long Island City, New York 11101

Scientific Flavors
2371 Beryllium Road
Scotch Plains, New Jersey 07076

Ultraviolet Light Stabilizer

Geigy Chemical Corp.
Saw Mill River Road
Ardsley, New York 10502
  Tinuvin.

CHANDLERS

Candle supplies can be purchased in arts and crafts shops and candle shops throughout America. The following are some mail-order suppliers.

Barker Enterprises
4208 S.W. 100th Street
Seattle, Washington 98146

The Candle Barn, Inc.
20 Sterling Road
Watchung, New Jersey 07060

The Candle Farm
625 South Church Street
Mount Laurel, New Jersey 08057

Candle-Makers Supply
630 N. College
Indianapolis, Indiana 46205

Fitzgerald Enterprises, Inc.
1610 E. 12th Street
Oakland, California 94604

General Supplies Co.
P.O. Box 338
Fallbrook, California 92028

Natcol Crafts, Inc.
P.O. Box 299
Redlands, California 92313

Novelcrafts Mfg. Co., Inc.
431 Rogue River Highway
Rogue River, Oregon 97537

Pinehurst Soap and Candle Co.
Pinehurst, North Carolina 28374

Pourette Mfg. Co.
6818 Roosevelt Way N.E.
Seattle, Washington 98115

Walco Products, Inc.
1200 Zerega Avenue
Bronx, New York 10462

Yaley Enterprises
358–D Shaw Road South
San Francisco, California 94080

DECORATION

Adhesive and Glaze

Mod-Podge
Brocado, Inc.
Chicago, Illinois 60608

Gold and Other Metallic Treatments

American Art Clay Co., Inc.
4010 W. 96th Street
Indianapolis, Indiana 46268
Rub'nBuff and Easy Leaf (Gold/Silver
Leaf).

American Wax Corp.
Azuza, California 91702
Whip-Wax.

Connoisseur Studio, Inc.
Louisville, Kentucky 40207
Treasure Gold.

EQUIPMENT

Electric Pen

Rapaport Bros., Inc.
500 N. Spaulding Avenue
Chicago, Illinois 60624
Rapco.

Melting Pot

Rival Manufacturing Co.
36 and Bennington
Kansas City, Missouri 64129
The Crock Pot.

Metal Stripping

Fred F. Wilcox Co., Inc.
Box 1056
Des Moines, Iowa 50311
Form-A-Frame, stainless steel.

Organic Vapors Mask

Pulmosan Safety Equipment Corp.
30–48 Linden Place
Flushing, New York 11354

MOLD MATERIALS

Adhesive Products Co.
1660 Boone Avenue
Bronx, New York 10460
   Adrub clear Stretchy Kwikset Rubber
   7169–2, 7170–1.

Dow Corning Corp.
Midland, Michigan 48640
   RTV Silicone: Silastic E.

General Electric Co.
Silicone Products Dept.
Waterford, New York 12188
   RTV Silicone: GE Silicones, RTV 630.

H. V. Hardman Co., Inc.
600 Cortlandt Street
Belleville, New Jersey 07109
   Kalex, a flexible material.

Marblette Corp.
37–21 30th Street
Long Island City, New York 11101
   Epoxies.

Pariscraft—a Johnson & Johnson Co.
P.O. Box 30
New Brunswick, New Jersey 08903
   Pariscraft plaster bandage.

Ren Plastics, Inc.
Lansing, Michigan 48909
   Epoxies.

WAX

Arco
Atlantic Richfield Co.
260 S. Broad Street
Philadelphia, Pa. 19107

Mobil
50 W. 44th Street
New York, New York 10036
   Fully refined, 145°F.

Frank B. Ross Co., Inc.
6 Ash Street
Jersey City, New Jersey 07304
   Prepared mixtures of candlemaking wax,
   Ross Compound 15–51 and beeswax.

Shell
Petrochemicals Division
1212 Avenue of the Americas
New York, New York 10036
   Mixed paraffins, 156°F.

WICKING

The Atkins and Pierce Mfg. Co.
Pearl and Pike streets
Cincinnati, Ohio 45202

Deep Flex Plastic Molds, Inc.
Box 11471
Fort Worth, Texas 76110
   Key Wick.

Index

(*Italic* figures refer to illustrations.)